GIFTS for WILD WOMEN

Alla,
Happy
Days

Robin

ISBN 0-9580742-1-6

CIP
1. Self-actualization (Psychology). 2. Conduct of life - Miscellanea.
3. Self-esteem in women. 4. Self-perception in women. 1. Title.

Published by EARTHCARE EDUCATION
                58 Crystal Waters
                M.S.16. Maleny.
                Q'ld. 4552 Australia.
Phone 61 (0)7 5494 4707   Email <robin@earthcare.com.au>

Cover Painting by Ember Kate Fairbairn

Illustrations by Jenny Kemp, Rebecca Hopkins, Andrew Clifford & Annette Muller

Border Designs by Nicole Brown

Cover Design and Formatting by Jenny Kemp and Robin Clayfield

Text Formatting and Layout by Robin Clayfield

Digital Photography of Author and Wild Woman by Hans Erken

Proofreading, review & feedback by Barry Goodman, Amber & Rebecca Hopkins

Proudly Printed in Australia on 100% Recycled Paper (to save trees).

Printing by Harding Colour (in Q'ld, Australia)
Using a Thread Sewn Binding (so it won't fall apart).

GIFTS for WILD WOMEN

By ROBIN CLAYFIELD

PUBLISHED BY EARTHCARE EDUCATION
MALENY, Q'LD, AUSTRALIA.

ALSO BY ROBIN CLAYFIELD

You Can Have Your Permaculture and Eat It Too

BY ROBIN CLAYFIELD and SKYE

Manual For Teaching Permaculture Creatively
Patterns In Nature Card Game
Principles Of Permaculture Card Game
Soils Roleplay Kit

ALL PUBLISHED BY EARTHCARE EDUCATION

DEDICATION

To all my Wild Women friends who have supported, nurtured and encouraged me on my journey to wholeness and beauty.

To the Wild Men in my life who, among other things, have gifted to me the opportunity to fully stand in my true power.

To my Wild Children who help me learn to love unconditionally and challenge me to find my 'centre' (in every moment?).

MAY WILD WOMEN'S WISDOM WEAVE A WEB OF WONDER AROUND THE WORLD.

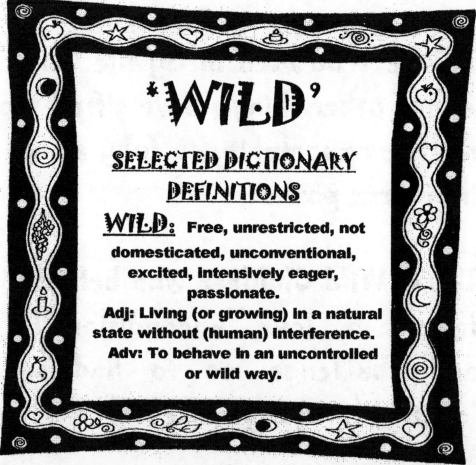

'WILD'

SELECTED DICTIONARY DEFINITIONS

WILD: Free, unrestricted, not domesticated, unconventional, excited, intensively eager, passionate.

Adj: Living (or growing) in a natural state without (human) interference.

Adv: To behave in an uncontrolled or wild way.

'WILD WOMEN'S WEEKEND' DEFINITIONS

WHAT DOES WILD MEAN TO YOU?

NOT CARING WHO SEES.

RELEASING.

WILD ABANDONMENT.

Being responsible for others and responsible for ourselves.

INSTINCT.

Freedom To Be....

MAD, MAYHEM, MIRTH.

freedom of Expression.

END FEAR.

PRIMAL.

TO HAVE FUN.

JUST TO BE.

Release Express Enjoy

To be yourself.

Being naked in nature with a beautiful snake draped around me.

To Be Creative

LIVE IT. LOVE IT. LIKE THERE'S NO TOMORROW. YEH!

Total Trust.

WILD IS BEST!

DANCE LIKE NO-ONE'S WATCHING

Take Massive Risks. (Like spin the bottle.)

S C R E E T C H

RUN FREE

As The Wind Does.

To love others.

NO MASKS

TO BE ABLE TO...

Love Me

LET IT ALL HANG OUT! Warts, Wrinkles, Droopy Bits, Hairy Bits and All

M.M.M.M......Pleasure.

Sleep. Itch. Eat. Fart.

Totally Uninhibited

Unchain My Heart, Set Me Free.

To Express Myself Without Restriction Or Expectation.

Yaba-daba-dooooo!

Dream It, Think It, Do It.

Throwing care to the wind.

Thank You to the Rockhampton 'Wild Women's Wisdom Weekend' for these beautiful responses.

3

CONTENTS

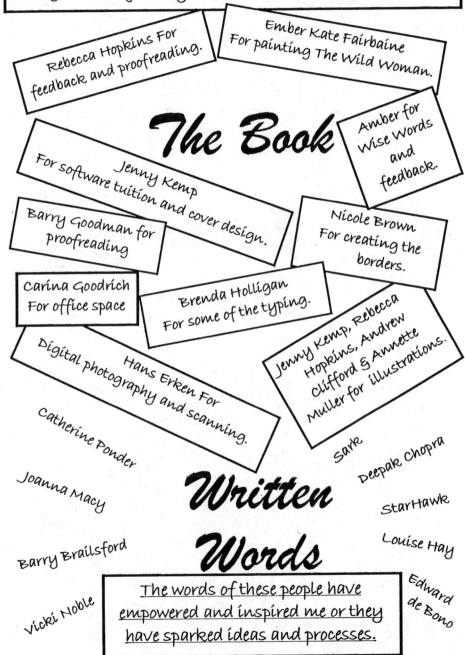

I acknowledge and give a very deep Thank You to all who have given me help, support, love, feedback and inspiration through out the journey and eventual birthing of this book.

Rebecca Hopkins For feedback and proofreading.

Ember Kate Fairbaine For painting The Wild Woman.

The Book

Amber for Wise Words and feedback.

Jenny Kemp For software tuition and cover design.

Barry Goodman for proofreading

Nicole Brown For creating the borders.

Carina Goodrich For office space

Brenda Holligan For some of the typing.

Jenny Kemp, Rebecca Hopkins, Andrew Clifford & Annette Muller for illustrations.

Hans Erken For Digital photography and scanning.

Catherine Ponder

Sark

Deepak Chopra

Joanna Macy

StarHawk

Written Words

Louise Hay

Barry Brailsford

Edward de Bono

Vicki Noble

The words of these people have empowered and inspired me or they have sparked ideas and processes.

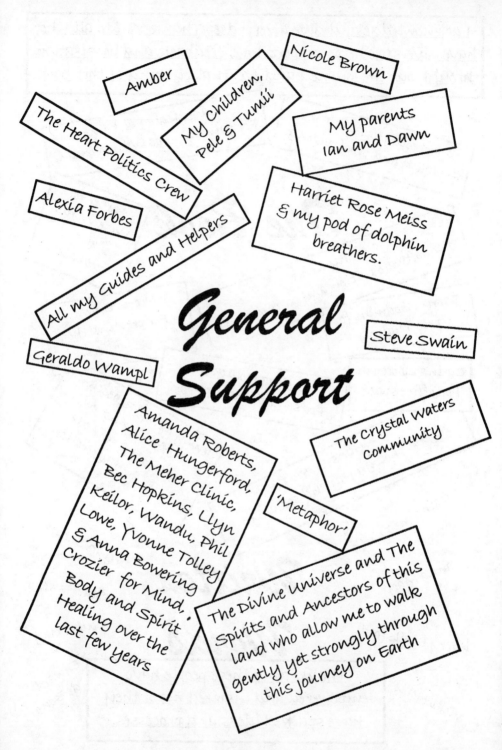

Amber

Nicole Brown

My Children, Pele & Tumii

The Heart Politics Crew

My parents Ian and Dawn

Alexia Forbes

Harriet Rose Meiss & my pod of dolphin breathers.

All my Guides and Helpers

General Support

Steve Swain

Geraldo Wampl

Amanda Roberts, Alice Hungerford, The Meher Clinic, Bec Hopkins, Llyn Keilor, Wandu, Phil Lowe, Yvonne Tolley & Anna Bowering Crozier for Mind, Body and Spirit Healing over the last few years

The Crystal Waters Community

'Metaphor'

The Divine Universe and The Spirits and Ancestors of this land who allow me to walk gently yet strongly through this journey on Earth

Jenny Allen

Zjamal Xanitha

Skye

John Seed

Eshana

(Dr Elizabeth Bragg)

Tracy Adams

Phil Lowe

Wronka Schneider-Ludorff

Djangawu

Amber

Joanna Macy

Amrita Hobbs

Evie Pickler

Harriet Rose Meiss

Friends, Co-Creators & Facilitators

Guboo Ted Thomas

De Sier

Robina McCurdy

Sue Fitzsimmons

Rob Swain

Those I've worked, played, and learnt with over the years and I feel are in some way connected with the seeds contained in this book.

AUTHOR'S NOTE - DISCLAIMER.

'Gifts For Wild Women' is offered as a source book of processes and ideas to help you, the reader, access more completely your wild, creative, intuitive, adventurous, divine, holistic nature.

In all cases where journeys, adven tures and activities are suggested please take full responsibility for yourself, take care and stay safe.

This book is not meant to be prescriptive in any way. If you have or suspect you have any medical or emotional problems be sure to seek appropriate m edical advice before embarking on any new process, project, adventure or healing modality.

Suggestions of healing treatments or herbs to use are guidelines only. Please also seek medical advice first if you've never used them before or if you're not 100% sure. The author and publisher cannot accept responsibility for any illness or injury arising from failure by the reader to seek medical advice.

While I encourage you to use this book fully, if anything doesn't feel right – don't do it. Be your own guide. Be aware, open and in your 'knowing'. Protect yourself energetically if you need to. Most importantly

– Relax and Enjoy.

HERSTORY
- AN INTRODUCTION

It's been a long journey! From teenage rebellion, mind, body and spirit numbing indulgences and a long period of low self esteem to deep connectedness, balance, beauty and bliss.

When I was 22 and just starting to feel like an adult, an astrologer told me that by the time I was middle aged I would be nicely balanced. Being a Libran I remember feeling quite dismayed that I would have to wait so long to achieve a state where everything in and around me was in perfect harmony. That was over 20 years ago and I can honestly say that most days I give thanks for, and celebrate, the balance, harmony and perfectness in my life.

I could choose to see many situations as problems, dramas or distractions yet I'm becoming more and more able to treat these things as challenges, tests and opportunities to grow, develop, renew and move forward. This has helped me immensely in maintaining a positive outlook rather than getting caught up in other peoples problems or my own mental and emotional baggage.

12 years of using B.R.E.T.H.work and a wide variety of other techniques, information and self-empowerment tools has greatly assisted me to clear this 'baggage' so I can now be responsive rather than reactive, living each moment as it comes and enjoying my life to the fullest.

This book is also a gift of 'Ross River Fever', a mosquito

borne body challenge that (over 6 years and 3 bouts of it) has helped me learn to <u>BE</u> and not <u>DO</u> so much.

I have worked (and played) teaching groups of people in Permaculture, Creative Facilitation and Empowerment for well over a Decade. In that time I've developed, adapted, borrowed, moulded, and created processes to suit the needs of the group or individual I'm involved with. 'Gifts For Wild Women' reflects and weaves together this development of processes and the tools that have worked for me as I've experienced my awakening.

I felt very guided throughout the creation of this book and the accompanying cards. Each process has worked for me and many of them have been used by other women who have also found them helpful.

As each card became a reality and blended into a set of 80, I felt very strongly that I was also being given an amazing gift, a gift from the universe. In turn I can now offer this set of processes to you in the hope that they may help you on your journey as they have helped me. As I write this I realise what a gift my whole life has been. I give thanks for the ease, prosperity, joy, health, abundance, creativity, spontaneity, harmony, wisdom, truth and love that flows into my life. I honour, acknowledge and thank all my guides, helpers, protectors, the spirits and ancestors of this, my land and my family, friends and community for being such a valuable and supportive presence.

And to you, beautiful reader, I wish a joyous and abundant life and <u>**may all your dreams come true**</u>.

LIVE EACH MOMENT

In this life I live each moment,
Letting go of all resistance
I let go my fears of past and future.

In this life I'm loving and joyful
Caring, sharing, flowing, growing,
Knowing I am wise and wonderful.

In this life I honor my spirit,
Knowing I am one with all things,
Going deep within myself and others

In this life I celebrate living,
Playing, laughing, loving, being,
Giving thanks for all that I am given.

In this life I vividly imagine
Each of us as crafty spiders
Spinning webs of love and weaving wonder.

Robin Clayfield 1999

spinning webs of love and weaving wonder!

After I wrote this song I realized that it was a statement which honored how I was feeling about my life. It is also a gift for me to sing when I need reminding during challenging times. To me it expresses the essence of this book. I hope you'll join me in each and every moment spinning webs of love and weaving wonder.   YEH!

HOW TO USE THIS BOOK

YOUR JOURNEY

'Gifts for Wild Women' offers you a journey to the depths of yourself by exploring a wondrous relationship with the most important person in your life - YOU. If you can give yourself love, honesty and compassion you'll be more able to give it freely to others.

This book is a tool to help you begin (or further assist you to continue) giving to yourself in a creative, constructive, beautiful and powerful way.

There are 80 processes, each one an adventure, a gift, a magical step in your journey to a more meaningful, balanced, joyous and fulfiling life.

BOOK AND CARD SET

As an empowerment tool this book is accompanied by 80 cards, yet I felt strongly that the book needed to stand alone so that it was more financially available to all women. If you have the boxed set of both the cards and the book, take a moment to sit quietly. When you feel ready, simply shuffle the cards asking "What do I most need to give myself at the moment?" Cut the cards twice and select the first one off the top. Alternatively, spread the cards out and pick the one you feel most drawn to as you're asking the same question.

You could even spread them out in a circle and spin a bottle or stick around to point at the card to pick. Experiment!

MAKING YOUR OWN CARDS

IF you have the book by itself you can ask your question and open the book anywhere. It is preferable though to make your own set of cards by selecting some coloured cardboard and cutting 80 cards small enough to be held in the hands and shuffled. A stamp, sticker or picture could be placed on the back of each one or maybe the cardboard could have a pattern on it already. Number the cards from 1 to 80. If you are really keen you could go through the book and copy the corresponding gift instruction onto each card.

Easy Option

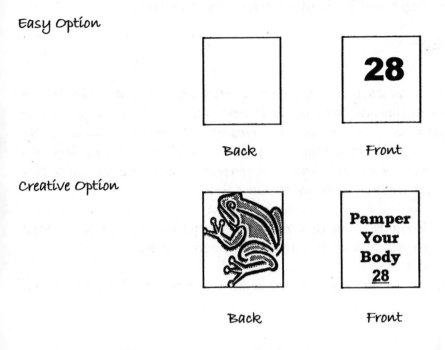

Back   Front

Creative Option

Back   Front

CREATE ADDITIONAL CARDS

For those of you with the card and book set you'll notice that there are two extra cards without writing. These are Masters/Mistresses in case you wish to copy more.

For those of you with the book only you'll find in the back of the book two blank master/mistress pages for you to photocopy onto cardboard (200gsm will go through some photocopiers) so you can add more gifts to the set if you want. Take some quiet time to brainstorm all the techniques, processes and tools that you've used or been guided through that have really helped you get to where you are now. All of the eighty cards in this set are examples yet I'm sure you'll think of other things that have worked for you in the past.

Write them onto the photocopied cards or format the words on a computer and print them out onto cardboard. You may also like to create cards for other things that you can think of to treat yourself to that neither of us have experienced. I'd love to hear your feedback of additions you've made and in fact any feedback about this book would be most welcome.

GLOSSARY

I've included a Glossary of Terms and Concepts and placed it in the front of the book rather than the back as most books do. I felt it was important for you to understand how I've used the words now rather than find out at the end or have to flip to the back if you're not clear on the meaning of a particular word. We all use language differently and place our cultural and sub-cultural glasses on when we read and write.

I hardly referred to a dictionary when compiling the glossary. Most definitions are my own understanding or interpretation

I encourage you to read it before you begin the book. Hopefully it will whet your appetite.

THEMES

I noticed through the process of writing up the gift cards that they fitted into a variety of themes.

▷   Body Honouring
▷   Earth and Garden
▷   Solo Adventures
▷   Connecting With Others
▷   Food - The Gift of Life
▷   The Written Word
▷   Personal Empowerment Tools
▷   Enjoying Creativity
▷   Rituals and Visual Journeys
▷   Purchases and Prosperity

We are multi-faceted beings who need diversity in our lives. By using a variety of ways to care for ourselves we add spice and excitement to our adventure on this planet

Creating the time and space to honour, nurture and give to yourself will hopefully bring harmony, balance and sustenance to your daily life while adding positive fuel to your personal contribution to our world, your connection with others and most importantly your connection with yourself.

ENJOY, PLAY, CREATE, GET OUT AND ABOUT, LIVE, LOVE

To me the bottom line is LOVE.

Some of the processes in this book may challenge you. They may trigger painful memories, fears or other emotions. Just remember to LOVE YOUR-SELF (sounds easy doesn't it). Do your 'work' with whatever comes up for you, move through these opportunities and receive the gift at the end.

Some processes are more challenging than others. A few are quite simple. Others require forethought and planning while others need financing. All of them will help you grow if you intend it to be so.

PLAY WITH THE CARDS WITH OTHERS

You may like to gather some of your friends together and during a ceremony or over a cup of tea choose a card each and offer to support each other to live out the instruction.

GIVE YOURSELF ALL THE GIFTS

Another way you may like to play with these processes is to read the book from cover to cover. Pick out all the ideas that you feel you most need to use or explore and create a plan to action them Alternatively, give yourself all the gifts one by one, then do it all over again, and again ... and don't stop.

P.S. For Men

This is a women's empowerment tool and as such has been designed for women. Men could equally benefit by its use and there is very little that is strictly women's business. So let the guys know that they don't need to feel left out and that they are welcome to try out anything here that feels comfortable and appropriate. You may like to include your male friends in some of the activities and processes. That's up to you. Maybe you could use some of these gifts to give to a male partner, friend or relative.

NETWORKING

I mentioned earlier that I'd love feedback about other processes that have worked for you, and about this book and card set. I feel strongly that as women, earthcarers and powerful change agents within society we can support each other and promote positive change in the world by networking and 'talking up' the good things that are available 'out there' in the world.

When I wrote and published my first book I had to learn to 'sell myself' (pretty scary at the time). I now gently and openly ask that if you felt gifted by the tools in this book or get a good feeling about my work please pass on your good P.R. to friends and mention my courses and workshops to others who may benefit or be interested. I've included some promotional material about my work at the back of the book.

I invite you to send me information in a similar vein so I can do the same for you. In this way we strengthen the amazing, colourful and dynamic web of women around the world who are working for change by doing their inner work at the same time.

THANK YOU FOR YOUR SUPPORT

I trust you will enjoy giving to yourself as you play with this book.

TERMS AND CONCEPTS
(sometimes called a Glossary).

Aerobic Activity. An activity or exercise, which stimulates breathing and strengthens the heart and lungs. At least 30 minutes of breathing with a heart rate of approximately 120 to 140 beats per minute 4 times a week is a suggested minimum amount to maintain an aerobic condition though everyone has individual differences.

Affirmation. A positive statement about oneself or the world around us that can be spoken as if it is happening now. A powerful way to change negative self-talk and belief systems and to manifest what we truly want and deserve in our lives.

Altar. A table, bench or object adorned and used in a sacred way. It could be as simple as a smooth stone or piece of driftwood in nature or as elaborate as a carved wooden table covered in a delicate bejeweled cloth. Candles, natural and sacred objects, talismans and symbols are placed on the altar, often in a ritualised and symbolic way.

Animal Totems. These are animals, either tangible or of the dreamworld, which a person may feel 'connected' to, guided by, or drawn to throughout their life. Emulating them, being guided by their characteristics or simply being close to them may bring lessons, new wisdom and comfort.

Astringent. A substance that tones the skin by drawing the pores together.

Bio-Region. A Biological region that is bounded by water, mountains, or other natural and sometimes unnatural features like highways. Your Bio-Region is one where you feel at home, which may have a central town or focus and where most trading and social interaction takes place for the people that live in that area.

Body Electronics. A healing science developed by John Whitman

Ray which combines nutrition, nutrient saturation, iris and sclera diagnosis and 'point holding' (a sustained accupressure) to bring about consciousness change and physical, mental and emotional healing.

Brainstorm. The simple process of allowing the mind to spark with ideas without limiting or thinking too much about them. Typically, a question is asked and the person or group offers the ideas which spontaneously come to mind. No answer is right or wrong and the process is kept moving so the answers are more intuitive than thought out or planned.

BRETHwork Similar to what's often called Rebirthing, BRETHwork uses a special breathing technique as the predominant tool to connect a person with their true inner self. Destructive cyclic patterns, childhood traumas, past life experiences and unhealed emotional pain can all be seen, realised, remembered, understood, cleansed, released and healed. B.R.E.T.H.work is undertaken in 'Sacred Space' with a trained 'Sitter' or facilitator setting it up and 'sitting ' with the person during a session.

Chai. The name for tea in India. It is traditionally spiced up with either ginger, cardamon, cinnamon, star anise, cloves or bay leaves. For a decadent western version use low tannin tea, add all the spices at once, grate in fresh ginger and bring to the boil. Add milk and bring back to the boil then sweeten with honey. This double brewing process gives the best results.

Chakras. A series of seven (or twelve) wheels of energy through the centre of the body. The Base Chakra is located at the coccyx at the base of the spine with the others in sequence up through the centre of the body to the Crown Chakra just above the top of the head.

Creative Facilitation. The opposite to a boring lecture (where the teacher, speaker or presenter uses speaking and a blackboard or whiteboard to deliver information to a group). Creative Facilitation is what it implies - creative ways to help people learn, take in information or achieve a task. The person facilitating empowers the group or individual by using a wide variety of fun, interactive and stimulating learning methods and processes which are more likely to have an impact and be remembered.

Deep Ecology. A way of thinking and living in an ecological way where we are all intimately and deeply connected to all beings and elements around us. Very different from viewing humans as the crown of creation.

Divination. Using tools such as cards, runes, tealeaves, pendulums... to gain answers to pertinent questions or find out about the future.

Essential Oils. Oil extracted from a plant, root or flower that is 100% pure. That is, it has not been diluted in any way or mixed with other oils or ingredients.

Elements. Often considered as AIR, FIRE, WATER and EARTH. Some belief systems and cultures include METAL and/or WOOD while most hold SPIRIT as the uniting force. These are often represented on an Altar or a circle centrepiece and can be aligned with the direction they symbolise, which can vary depending on cultural, religious or personal leanings.

Empowerment. The state or process of being clearly, strongly and confidently able to do something. Working with ones own authority and feeling good about it.

'First Voice, Best Voice'. A way of working with your intuition where you ask yourself a question (or someone else asks you) and you accept the first thing that comes into your mind as the answer (without thinking). That's usually your intuition, the voice of your higher self.

Food Combining. Mixing different foods in combinations that are compatible. In this way food is digested properly, there is no wind or indigestion and nutrients have a good chance of being absorbed. A classic example is eating grapes or melons alone.

'Four Directions'. In Native American and other indigenous cultures the four directions (east, north, west and south) are honoured for the unique gifts and attributes that each bring to the circle or 'wheel of life'. Each individual stands with spirit, in the centre of his or her own circle.

Gestalt. Developed by Fritz Perls, this healing technique allows a person to see and speak from the many aspects of themselves to relieve the sub-conscious mind of traumatic burdens by bringing them to the surface for counselling and clearing.

Grounded/Ungrounded. Being grounded is the feeling of being solid, connected to Earth and Spirit and able to assimilate and use the wisdom and guidance from the higher realms. If we're ungrounded we may feel floaty, scattered, unprotected, lightheaded and not able to fully connect to earth or implement guidance or visions.

Heart Centre. That space in the centre of your chest often referred to as the Heart (or 4th) Chakra.

Higher Self. The part of ourselves that is connected to Spirit and that we can ask for guidance and receive knowing, wise answers. Its' home and access point is the crown chakra. Focusing our energy there and out to Spirit can help and support this connection.

Highest Good. The very best, most positive outcome for you, all beings and the planet. It can be a very clear and powerful message to both yourself and the Universe to weave this in when working with 'Intention' and Manifesting.

Intention. Consciously and clearly setting in place in our minds and hearts the intention that something will take place or change in our lives. This is very powerful energy work and can be part of every action even in our daily living. To sweep the floor is one thing. To sweep the floor having in mind that with every stroke unwanted thoughts, emotions, ill health, clutter etc is swept out of our lives is a very strong message to our sub-conscious. To place a circle on the ground knowing that every time we step into it we step into quiet contemplation and sacred space helps this to be so.

22

Kahuna Massage. A traditional Hawaiian form of massage where the masseuse uses flowing, sweeping movements and strokes with their whole arm and elbow. Kahuna is a wholistic philosophy and way of life, with massage being only a component. Definitely the most powerful and dynamic type of massage I've ever had.

Kinesiology. A healing modality that utilises muscle testing and the body's meridian system to identify health problems and restore balance, health and vitality.

'Knowing'. Your intuition. That part of yourself that just knows something is about to happen or that it's your best friend on the phone. The 'Wise Woman' part of yourself.

Rebounder. A small round trampoline which when used helps stimulate the lymphatic system. Sometimes also called a Lymphasizer.

Manifest. To create, attract, bring about that which you want in your life or for the planet. In this context it is a conscious invitation released to the Universe with ·pure intention, and made without neediness or attachment.

Mandala. A pattern with a central focus that generally radiates out in a symmetrical fashion.

Marimba. A traditional African instrument that looks like a big wooden xylophone. Gourds are often suspended underneath each note to resonate the sound. Some modern versions use slotted Agricultural pipe or downpipe as resonators.

Medicine Wheel. A Native American concept, where life is a sacred circle, a sacred medicine wheel that is protected by and encompasses the spirits and energies of the four directions. Above, Below and Within (Spirit) are also acknowledged and honoured as part of this system. A Medicine wheel can be physically created with a ring of stones, objects, a round structure or tobacco pouches as are sometimes used traditionally. The four directions are 'Called In' (invited, invoked) and ceremony, ritual, sacred work or vision questing is undertaken. The wheel can be large enough for a whole tribe/mob/family or it can be small enough for only one person depending on the purpose of the circle.

Meridian System. This is the whole energetic circulatory system of the body according to Eastern tradition. There is a governing meridian that looks after the overall health of the body, then there are liver, gall bladder, kidney, stomach...and other meridians. There are key points, called pressure points along each meridian. Shiatsu, Acupuncture and acupressure all utilise the meridians as a basis for their healing systems.

Mulch. Any organic matter that is placed on a garden or around fruit trees and plants. It is used to help retain moisture in the soil, suppress weed growth, stabilise soil temperature and preserve the soil while also feeding it. Hay, straw, nut shells, compost, dead leaves, lawn clippings, old dried horse manure and spent mushroom compost are all good sources while living mulches can also be used alone or in addition to the non-living ones.

Muscle Testing. A process whereby the tester uses gentle pressure to push down (or in a specific direction) on a body part while asking a question or testing for a named weakness or deficiency. The receiver maintains resistance to the pressure. If the resistance holds it means that the muscle is strong and the answer positive (if asking a yes/no question). If the muscle gives way it is weak in relation to the question, indicating that maybe a whole meridian system is weak or that the answer is no. This is a beautiful, gentle way for our body to answer questions.

Nature Spirits. These are spirit beings that are not connected to specific plants but are more generally associated with and guardians for areas and elements of nature.

Networking. The powerful and dynamic process of sharing, exchanging, linking and developing contacts and connections between groups, organisations and individuals all around the world. A 'Grass

Roots' phenomena which is helping change the world for the better. Not to be confused with network marketing, or using the Internet.

NLP. Neuro-Linguistic Programming. A diverse healing modality which can assist people to track back to key or causal situations in their life which may still have an influence on daily wellbeing and relationships. N.L.P. also looks at how we learn and take in information and can help us reprogram our thoughts and actions.

Patterns. Ways of being or reacting to situations that seem to be cyclic, reappearing in our life regularly or in certain circumstances.

Perennial Plant. A plant that goes on growing, flowering and producing year after year. It doesn't die after one season as with an 'annual' plant.

Permaculture. A design system based on a range of common sense principles and ethics that are inspired by nature and natural systems. With these principles in mind, gardens, orchards, farms, buildings, communities, even financial and social systems can all be designed and implemented in a holistic, sensitive, productive, supportive and functional way.

Plant Divas. Each type of plant has a spirit being, or Diva that looks after it energetically. Each Diva is connected to the individual plants of that variety.

Pulsing. A healing modality where the practitioner deeply feels for the intrinsic natural vibrational pulse of the person, and gently rocks their whole body in tune with it. This 'Way of the water' profoundly heals deep early emotions, leaving the receiver calm, relaxed and freer in their body and lives.

Reflexology. Massage of the feet, especially the reflexology points, which are said to contain areas which relate to every other part of the body, so massaging the feet in effect works on the whole body.

Ritual. An action or series of processes done with ceremony and intent. Sacred space is usually created to begin with. A church service or the invoking of the 4 directions by Native Americans are two examples of traditional Rituals. A simple shower can become a ritual if you have the intent to cleanse off all unwanted energies and refresh yourself anew. Sweeping the floor can also be transformed from a menial task into a powerful cleansing.

Sacred. Anything felt to be special, blessed, divine, holy.

Sacred Objects. Any object, natural or manufactured, which has meaning or significance for the bearer and is used for the highest good of all concerned. Stones, feathers, gems, dolls, jewellery, bowls, beads, statues, ritual tools and instruments, food items, bones, cards, photos and pictures, any thing really. It is ideal to have a selection of these available for setting altars, sacred places and circle centre pieces as well as for creating gardens and gifts for others. A variety of cloths and covers is also recommended.

Sacred Space. Any place (in nature or a human creation) that is cleansed, blessed, acknowledged, honoured or used in a sacred way for ceremony, ritual, meditation, vision questing or other special activities. It is important to work with Intention when creating Sacred Space and to be in ones honour and humbleness when in such a place. A cushion in a corner, a bedroom or a religious shrine can all be Sacred Spaces in their own way.

Shiatsu. A healing modality from Japan similar to massage but where pressure points along the meridians of the body are pressed firmly rather than the body being rubbed as in massage.

Smudge Stick and Smudging. A bundle of herbs tied together while fresh and then dried. One end is them lit and the smoke used to cleanse a person's energy field, a room or house, a gathering or circle of people, even animals or sacred objects can be smudged. Traditionally sage, cedar and Sweet grass are used in North and Central America. Mugwort, Lavender,

Rosemary, Clary Sage and Geranium can all be used if they grow in your area. Australian Aboriginals use smoke from a fire for a similar purpose, while Catholic and other denominations use smoking herbs and incense sticks to cleanse and purify.

'Stuff' / 'Baggage'. Any pattern, idea, judgment, belief, emotion or burden that limits us or holds us back from awakening to our true potential. Once cleared we become more able to respond to life and daily situations rather than react, resent and restrict ourselves and others.

Tai Chi. An Eastern form of exercise more like a dance than a martial art. A very 'centreing' practise.

Talisman. An object, stone or carved symbol often carried on one's body, sometimes hidden, and used as a sacred object, good luck charm or source of extra power.

Tarot Cards. A divination tool that can give guidance to specific questions or life situations. Based on the original deck of playing cards each one has a meaning, the Court cards being related to major life issues while the others talk more about daily life. There are many versions available these days along with a huge variety of other divination cards, stones, coins etc. All of them are useful tools for helping to connect with inner knowing and wisdom. Before you draw a card, set the intention that whichever one you pick it will be what you most need to know at the moment.

Tithing. Giving a percentage of ones income, time and/or energy to a worthy or spiritual cause. 10% is often used and it is recommended that it is done anonymously and given freely with no expectations or ego involved.

Universe. All there is, including Spirit, Earth, other planets and galaxies. I think in terms of the Divine Universe and it is this power that I give thanks to for all that happens in my life. Sometimes I use the word in the context of asking support from or trusting the Universe to offer the perfect opportunities for me to learn, grow or be gifted what I need in life. I often 'hand it all over to the Universe to look after' at which point I 'let go' of fear and worry and simply trust.

Vision Quest. An experience or journey, often up to four days long, where a person finds a place in nature to use as a retreat space. Visions and visits by animals and spirit beings are common, especially when the person has fasted and prepared for this special time and undertaken the journey with the intent to grow, learn, see and experience more of their true power, potential and connection to spirit.

Visualisation/Visual journey. An experience, self-guided or guided by another, in which the higher self and Spirit can be clearly and easily accessed. (It can take a little while for some people to fully 'see' during the experience.) Positive outcomes, life dreams and future hopes can be seen and explored, helping them to happen more easily. Healing can also be powerfully assisted through positive visual images. Clearing and emotional release can be gently introduced while messages and guidance related to life situations and general wellbeing are a common focus. I find visualisations to be an extremely powerful tool for change, empowerment and creative learning.

Voice Dialogue. A healing process in which a facilitator assists the client to engage in dialogue between different aspects of themselves and with significant others so they can realise and clear out past traumas and blockages.

Watsu. Water Shiatsu. A gentle, soothing and releasing massage where you are cradled, floated and worked on by the practicioner in a pool heated to body temperature.

' Witness '. The part of us that watches our movements and thoughts objectively and alerts us to our own negative self talk, judgments, reactions, ego outbursts... She also keeps us safe and grounded on B.R.E.T.H. Journeys, out of body experiences and moments of expanded emotion. Our 'Witness' is often silenced or ignored in the current mayhem of modern society but she can be reawakened.

THE
GIFTS

FEED YOURSELF LOVE LIGHT and HAPPINESS

<u>1</u>

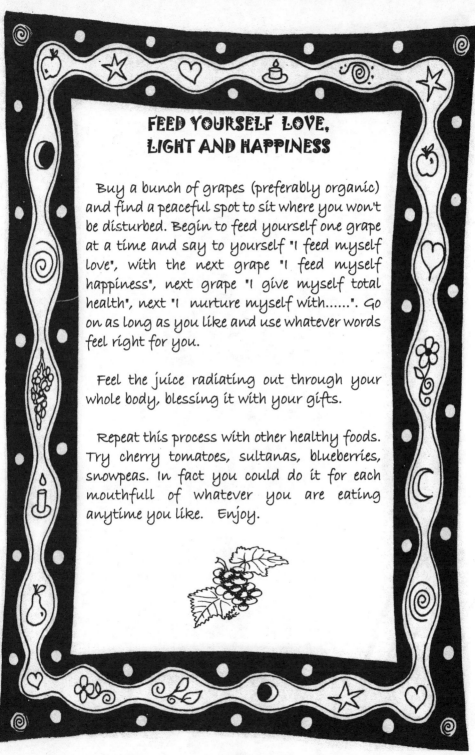

FEED YOURSELF LOVE, LIGHT AND HAPPINESS

Buy a bunch of grapes (preferably organic) and find a peaceful spot to sit where you won't be disturbed. Begin to feed yourself one grape at a time and say to yourself "I feed myself love", with the next grape "I feed myself happiness", next grape "I give myself total health", next "I nurture myself with......". Go on as long as you like and use whatever words feel right for you.

Feel the juice radiating out through your whole body, blessing it with your gifts.

Repeat this process with other healthy foods. Try cherry tomatoes, sultanas, blueberries, snowpeas. In fact you could do it for each mouthfull of whatever you are eating anytime you like. Enjoy.

MAKE A SACRED JOURNEY STICK

2

MAKE A
SACRED JOURNEY STICK

Go to a wild place and ask to be shown or led to a special stick or piece of driftwood. Sit with it awhile and get to know it then begin to attach colourful ribbons and cloth, feathers, shells, any sacred or meaningful objects that feel appropriate.

Work with the intent that each object signifies a strength that you need to be working with at this time. As you tie knots and attach objects feel yourself tying in Love for yourself, Confidence, Trust, Joy... Whatever you need more of in your life. Let the stick be your companion on your inner journey. Place it so that you will often see it and be reminded of all the things that you've woven into it. Take it with you to sacred gatherings and special events.

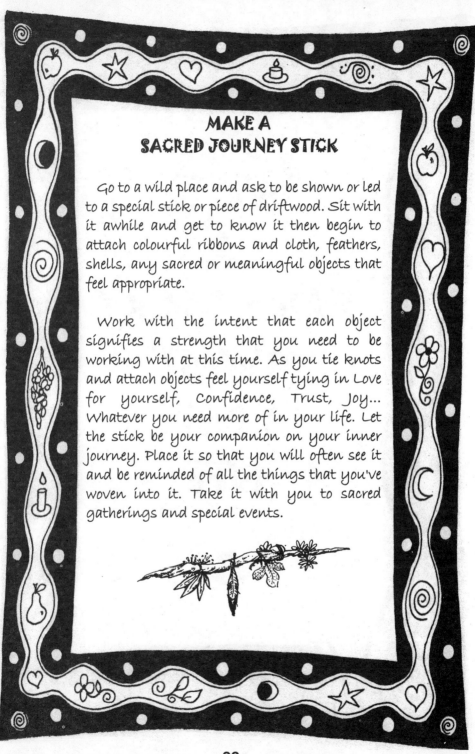

WRITE A FAIRY STORY ABOUT YOUR LIFE

3

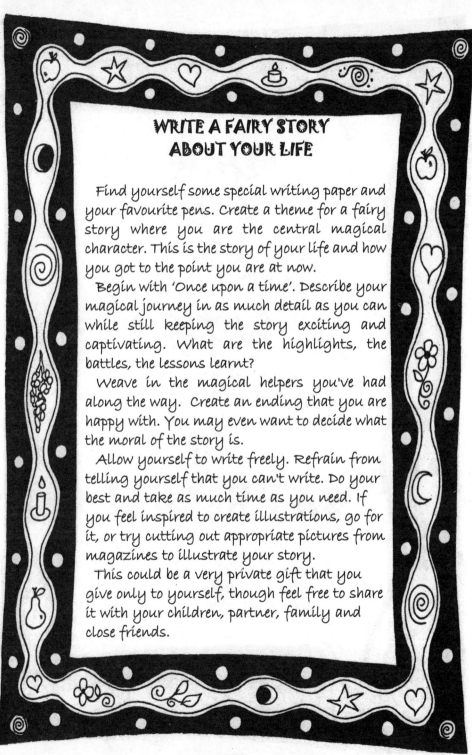

WRITE A FAIRY STORY
ABOUT YOUR LIFE

Find yourself some special writing paper and your favourite pens. Create a theme for a fairy story where you are the central magical character. This is the story of your life and how you got to the point you are at now.

Begin with 'Once upon a time'. Describe your magical journey in as much detail as you can while still keeping the story exciting and captivating. What are the highlights, the battles, the lessons learnt?

Weave in the magical helpers you've had along the way. Create an ending that you are happy with. You may even want to decide what the moral of the story is.

Allow yourself to write freely. Refrain from telling yourself that you can't write. Do your best and take as much time as you need. If you feel inspired to create illustrations, go for it, or try cutting out appropriate pictures from magazines to illustrate your story.

This could be a very private gift that you give only to yourself, though feel free to share it with your children, partner, family and close friends.

MAKE
EYE
CONTACT
WITH
PEOPLE
and
SAY HELLO!

4

MAKE EYE CONTACT WITH PEOPLE AND SAY HELLO

Say Hello to everyone who has eye contact with you today. Alternatively, give them a warm smile. Be especially conscious of doing this with your everyday family and friends.

If it feels okay find a way to strike up a conversation with strangers.

Be brave.

Be open to the beauty of other people.

Acknowledge what a gift a friendly smile and a kind word can be.

TAKE
A
MAGICAL
HOLIDAY

5

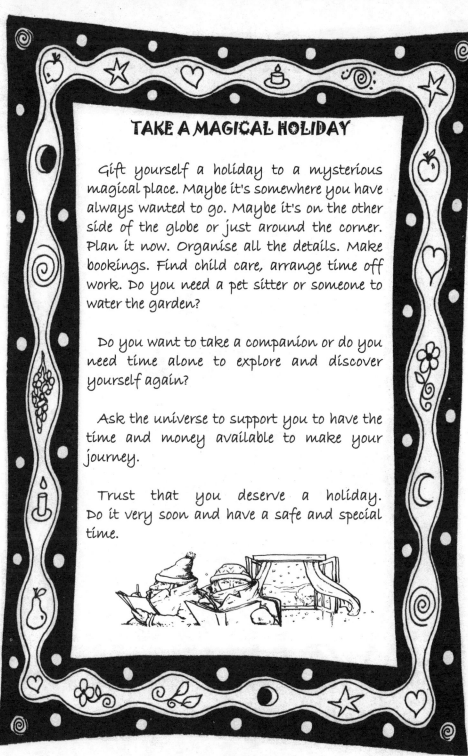

TAKE A MAGICAL HOLIDAY

Gift yourself a holiday to a mysterious magical place. Maybe it's somewhere you have always wanted to go. Maybe it's on the other side of the globe or just around the corner. Plan it now. Organise all the details. Make bookings. Find child care, arrange time off work. Do you need a pet sitter or someone to water the garden?

Do you want to take a companion or do you need time alone to explore and discover yourself again?

Ask the universe to support you to have the time and money available to make your journey.

Trust that you deserve a holiday. Do it very soon and have a safe and special time.

SHARE YOUR PERSONAL STORY

6

SHARE YOUR PERSONAL STORY

Arrange to meet with someone that you'd like to be much closer friends with but have never found the time or made the effort. Maybe you could send them an invitation to be your friend and to meet at your favourite coffee shop or somewhere more secluded. Ask them to allow plenty of time for your meeting.

Share with them your personal story. Give it as a gift that they may know you better. Then listen while they tell you theirs. Be 'In Your Truth' with them so that you have no hidden agendas, expectations or assumptions.

Thank them for sharing with you.

BUY YOURSELF A TEDDY BEAR

7

BUY YOURSELF A TEDDY BEAR

Visit Toy stores, craft shops, department stores or markets with the expressed purpose of buying yourself a teddy bear. Don't just take the first one that you find. Wait till one jumps out at you and says 'Take me home, I'm the one for you'.

Give it a name. Tell it your deepest, darkest fears and secrets. Hold it in times of grief, uncertainty or fear. Snuggle it when you feel touched by love or vulnerability.

You may even like to make clothes for it.

Most importantly, cuddle it regularly.

PAMPER YOUR BODY

8

PAMPER YOUR BODY

It's time to really treat yourself.

Pamper your body in ways you wouldn't normally think of doing.

Pick two gifts to give yourself from the list below.

▷Buy a skinbrush and brush yourself all over. Let it become a morning ritual before showering.

▷Have a massage or some reflexology (foot massage).

▷Receive a facial, preferably made from natural ingredients and essential oils.

▷Have a spa or a sauna.

▷Buy a new outfit made from fabric that is soft on the skin like velvet, satin, cashmere or soft cotton.

▷Indulge in a float tank experience.

▷Enjoy a pedicure (foot pampering) preceded by a foot bath.

Tell yourself that you deserve it.

DE-CLUTTER YOUR LIFE

9

DE-CLUTTER YOUR LIFE

Give yourself the gift of a clear fresh environment. De-cluttering brings your life into the present by letting go of the past.

Clean out all your cupboards, corners, spare rooms, under the bed...... It's time. Give away anything that you don't totally love or need in your life right now. If this task seems too huge, start with one corner or area and continue, one area at a time.

Be courageous.

Thank each item that you are clearing out. Appreciate what it has given you over the years or let go of the possibilities of (not) doing something with it in the future.

Make space for new things to enter your life and remember to give thanks and value them when they come.

LOOSEN UP WITH A TRANCE DANCE

10

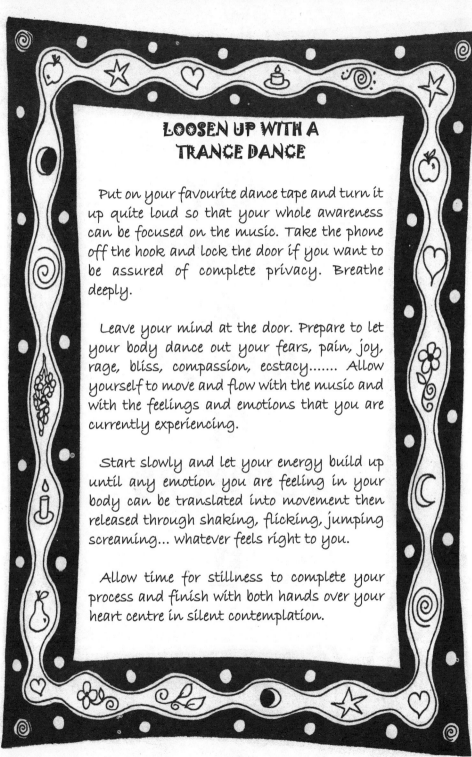

LOOSEN UP WITH A TRANCE DANCE

Put on your favourite dance tape and turn it up quite loud so that your whole awareness can be focused on the music. Take the phone off the hook and lock the door if you want to be assured of complete privacy. Breathe deeply.

Leave your mind at the door. Prepare to let your body dance out your fears, pain, joy, rage, bliss, compassion, ecstacy....... Allow yourself to move and flow with the music and with the feelings and emotions that you are currently experiencing.

Start slowly and let your energy build up until any emotion you are feeling in your body can be translated into movement then released through shaking, flicking, jumping screaming... whatever feels right to you.

Allow time for stillness to complete your process and finish with both hands over your heart centre in silent contemplation.

49

BUY YOURSELF A BUNCH OF FLOWERS

11

BUY YOURSELF
A BUNCH OF FLOWERS

Have you ever bought flowers for yourself? Now's the time. Search out a bunch of flowers to purchase from a florist, a roadside stall, the local market or maybe even the little old lady down the road with the amazing rose garden.

When you get home arrange them in a beautiful vase or divide them up and place in strategic spots around your house or room. Let them be a reflection and a reminder of your inner beauty.

You may instead choose to buy a perennial flowering plant in a pot from a nursery which will go on living and flowering each year.

Alternatively, go out into your own garden or a friend's and pick yourself a bouquet. Make it as colourful as you can and include some sprigs of scented herbs like lavender, rosemary or any of the geraniums. be sure to breathe deeply.

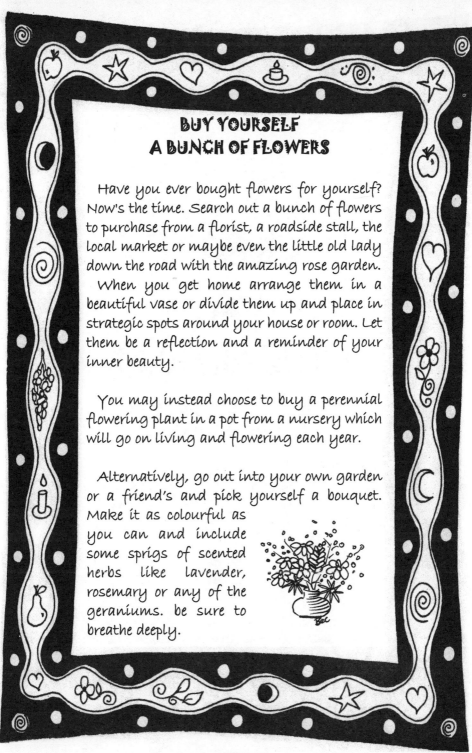

51

CREATE A COMMUNAL PICTURE

12

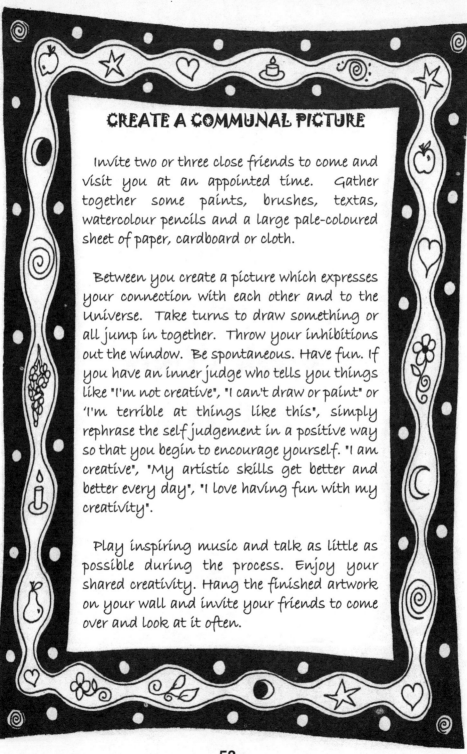

CREATE A COMMUNAL PICTURE

Invite two or three close friends to come and visit you at an appointed time. Gather together some paints, brushes, textas, watercolour pencils and a large pale-coloured sheet of paper, cardboard or cloth.

Between you create a picture which expresses your connection with each other and to the universe. Take turns to draw something or all jump in together. Throw your inhibitions out the window. Be spontaneous. Have fun. If you have an inner judge who tells you things like "I'm not creative", "I can't draw or paint" or 'I'm terrible at things like this", simply rephrase the self judgement in a positive way so that you begin to encourage yourself. "I am creative", "My artistic skills get better and better every day", "I love having fun with my creativity".

Play inspiring music and talk as little as possible during the process. Enjoy your shared creativity. Hang the finished artwork on your wall and invite your friends to come over and look at it often.

BEGIN A MORNING RITUAL

13

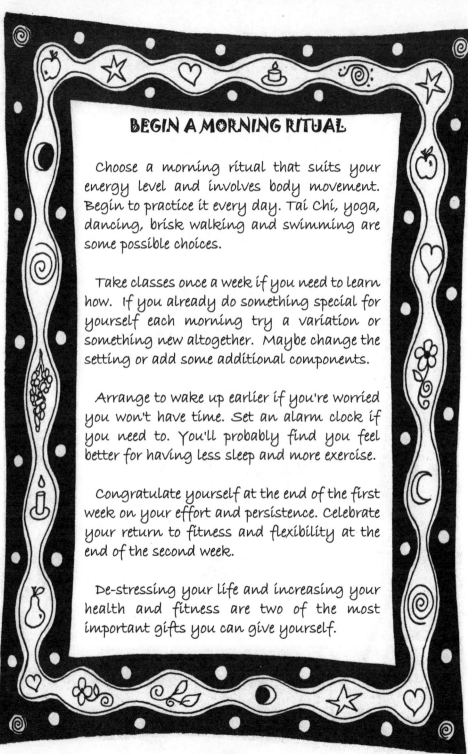

BEGIN A MORNING RITUAL

Choose a morning ritual that suits your energy level and involves body movement. Begin to practice it every day. Tai Chi, yoga, dancing, brisk walking and swimming are some possible choices.

Take classes once a week if you need to learn how. If you already do something special for yourself each morning try a variation or something new altogether. Maybe change the setting or add some additional components.

Arrange to wake up earlier if you're worried you won't have time. Set an alarm clock if you need to. You'll probably find you feel better for having less sleep and more exercise.

Congratulate yourself at the end of the first week on your effort and persistence. Celebrate your return to fitness and flexibility at the end of the second week.

De-stressing your life and increasing your health and fitness are two of the most important gifts you can give yourself.

TELL YOURSELF THAT YOU DESERVE THE BEST

14

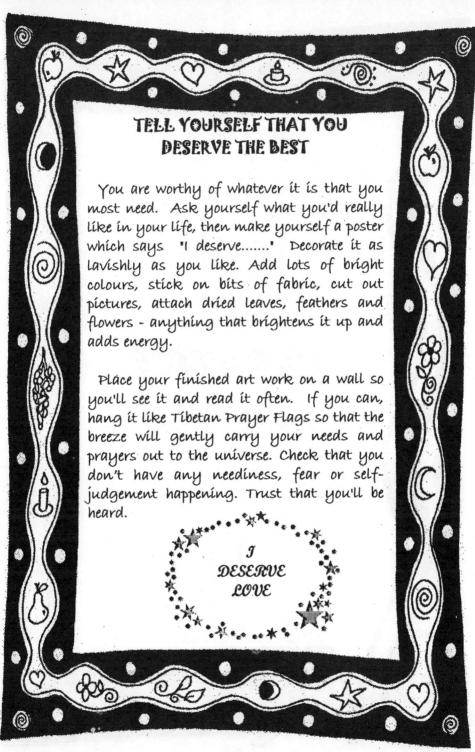

TELL YOURSELF THAT YOU DESERVE THE BEST

You are worthy of whatever it is that you most need. Ask yourself what you'd really like in your life, then make yourself a poster which says "I deserve......." Decorate it as lavishly as you like. Add lots of bright colours, stick on bits of fabric, cut out pictures, attach dried leaves, feathers and flowers - anything that brightens it up and adds energy.

Place your finished art work on a wall so you'll see it and read it often. If you can, hang it like Tibetan Prayer Flags so that the breeze will gently carry your needs and prayers out to the universe. Check that you don't have any neediness, fear or self-judgement happening. Trust that you'll be heard.

I DESERVE LOVE

BEGIN A CREATIVE PROJECT

15

BEGIN A CREATIVE PROJECT

Think about a creative project that you have been wanting to do for ages but have always put off.

Share with a friend about this project so you have someone to 'witness' what you're doing. It may also help you to clarify details if you can bounce your ideas off someone else.

If you're the sort of person who dreams up a big project, yet never quite manages to complete it, then choose a small project that only takes a few hours.

Gather together all the bits and pieces that you'll need. Buy and organise the materials. Create a space to set up for your project so that all the bits can be left out until completion.

Most importantly -
Do it now.

HAVE A HOT BATH

16

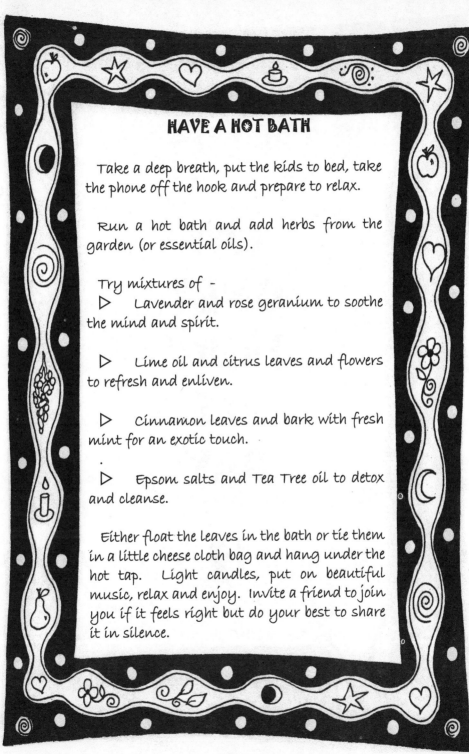

HAVE A HOT BATH

Take a deep breath, put the kids to bed, take the phone off the hook and prepare to relax.

Run a hot bath and add herbs from the garden (or essential oils).

Try mixtures of -
▷   Lavender and rose geranium to soothe the mind and spirit.

▷   Lime oil and citrus leaves and flowers to refresh and enliven.

▷   Cinnamon leaves and bark with fresh mint for an exotic touch.

▷   Epsom salts and Tea Tree oil to detox and cleanse.

Either float the leaves in the bath or tie them in a little cheese cloth bag and hang under the hot tap. Light candles, put on beautiful music, relax and enjoy. Invite a friend to join you if it feels right but do your best to share it in silence.

EAT
ONLY
FRUIT
ALL
DAY

17

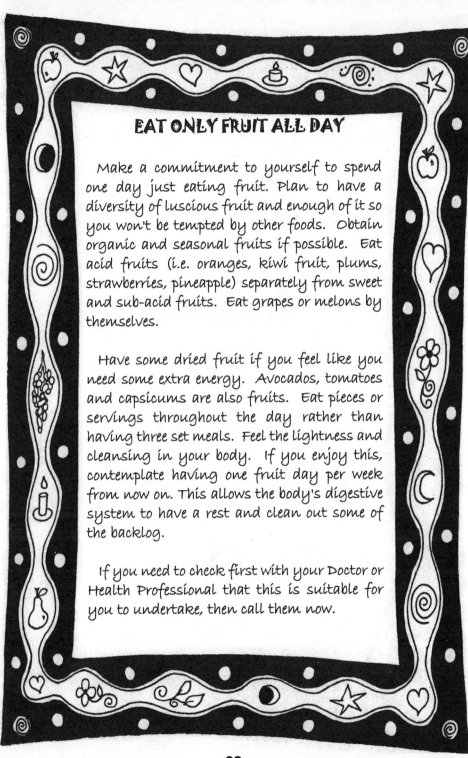

EAT ONLY FRUIT ALL DAY

Make a commitment to yourself to spend one day just eating fruit. Plan to have a diversity of luscious fruit and enough of it so you won't be tempted by other foods. Obtain organic and seasonal fruits if possible. Eat acid fruits (i.e. oranges, kiwi fruit, plums, strawberries, pineapple) separately from sweet and sub-acid fruits. Eat grapes or melons by themselves.

Have some dried fruit if you feel like you need some extra energy. Avocados, tomatoes and capsicums are also fruits. Eat pieces or servings throughout the day rather than having three set meals. Feel the lightness and cleansing in your body. If you enjoy this, contemplate having one fruit day per week from now on. This allows the body's digestive system to have a rest and clean out some of the backlog.

If you need to check first with your Doctor or Health Professional that this is suitable for you to undertake, then call them now.

BE SILENT IN NATURE

18

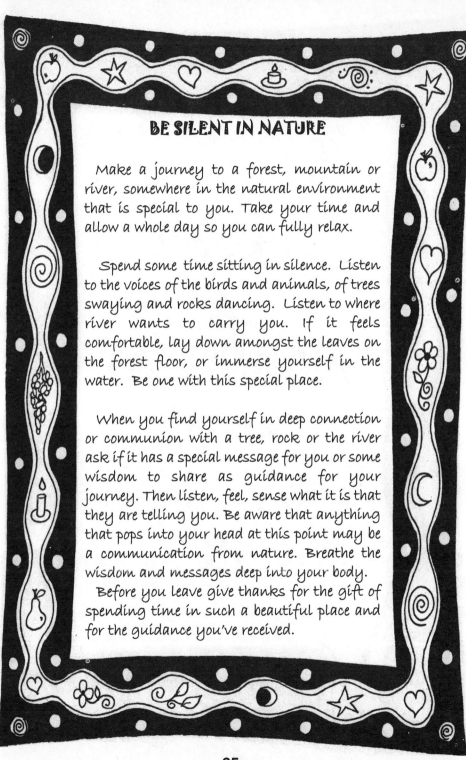

BE SILENT IN NATURE

Make a journey to a forest, mountain or river, somewhere in the natural environment that is special to you. Take your time and allow a whole day so you can fully relax.

Spend some time sitting in silence. Listen to the voices of the birds and animals, of trees swaying and rocks dancing. Listen to where river wants to carry you. If it feels comfortable, lay down amongst the leaves on the forest floor, or immerse yourself in the water. Be one with this special place.

When you find yourself in deep connection or communion with a tree, rock or the river ask if it has a special message for you or some wisdom to share as guidance for your journey. Then listen, feel, sense what it is that they are telling you. Be aware that anything that pops into your head at this point may be a communication from nature. Breathe the wisdom and messages deep into your body.

Before you leave give thanks for the gift of spending time in such a beautiful place and for the guidance you've received.

ENJOY
A
MOONLIGHT
SWIM

19

ENJOY A MOONLIGHT SWIM

Plan to swim and bathe in the light of the full moon. Wait till the moon is high overhead before you jump in. Be naked if you possibly can. It would be advisable to have a companion with you unless you know the water really well and feel 100% safe. Why not invite all your friends and have a moonlight skinny-dipping party.

If you can't possibly do this process, stand outside under the full moon and visualise strongly that you are floating in water, being enlivened, healed and cleansed by the power and beauty of the moon's light and the water's gentle touch.

Alternatively - Acquire an old bathtub and locate it in a private garden setting outside your home. Shape the ground so that the bath has a fire pit underneath which you can use to heat up the water anytime you feel like a hot bath especially on full moon nights. Place a mat or towel on the bottom so you don't burn your bum! If you've never had an outdoor bath experience it must be time to try it.

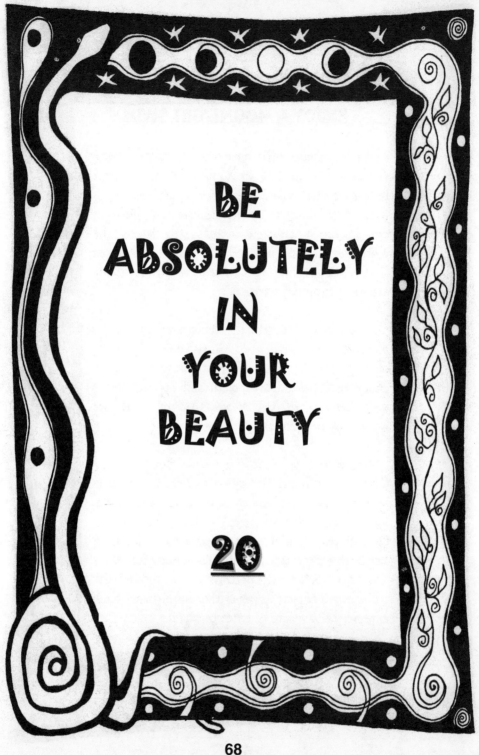

BE
ABSOLUTELY
IN
YOUR
BEAUTY

20

BE ABSOLUTELY IN YOUR BEAUTY

The most powerful way we can operate is to be absolutely in our centre, in our knowing, in our power and in our joy, our heart open, our chakras resonating, fully connected to our source energy, grounded, earthed and balanced. We need our guides, helpers, protectors and shields in place while having a clear mental and emotional body.

In this space we are in our absolute beauty. Find a special healer who can help awaken all of this in you and who can assist you to clear out anything that is unwanted or damaging. Ask yourself who the person is that can help. Alternatively, find a friend who can ask you about each of these things while you etherically adjust, mend, and call in whatever energies you need to.

You'll feel it when you're totally 'tuned up'. You may have specific colours that reside in different parts of your body and totem animals that make their home within and around you. Feel what these are and make sure they are in place. Remember to give thanks for this very special gift and each day check that everything is still in order.

CREATE
A
SACRED
SPACE

21

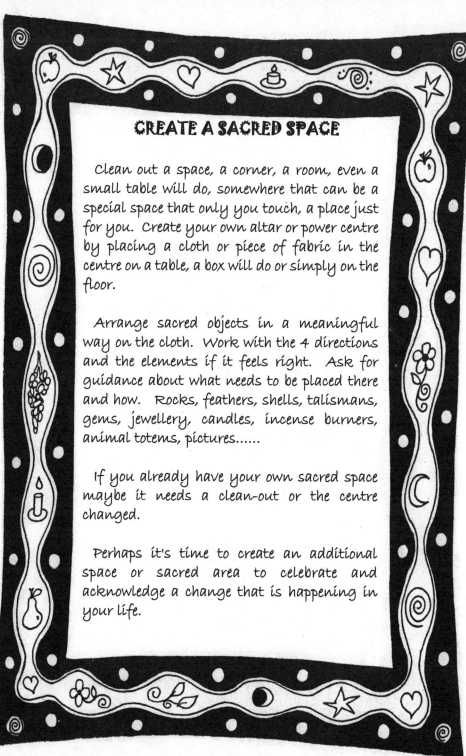

CREATE A SACRED SPACE

Clean out a space, a corner, a room, even a small table will do, somewhere that can be a special space that only you touch, a place just for you. Create your own altar or power centre by placing a cloth or piece of fabric in the centre on a table, a box will do or simply on the floor.

Arrange sacred objects in a meaningful way on the cloth. Work with the 4 directions and the elements if it feels right. Ask for guidance about what needs to be placed there and how. Rocks, feathers, shells, talismans, gems, jewellery, candles, incense burners, animal totems, pictures......

If you already have your own sacred space maybe it needs a clean-out or the centre changed.

Perhaps it's time to create an additional space or sacred area to celebrate and acknowledge a change that is happening in your life.

PERFORM A GIVEAWAY CEREMONY

22

PERFORM A GIVEAWAY CEREMONY

Invite a group of special friends to share in a giveaway ceremony. Arrange a time and place and ask each person to bring an object that is precious to them and symbolises something they want to let go of from their life. They need to be prepared to give the object away.

Sit together in a circle. To begin, create sacred space in any way that feels appropriate and invite in any energies, helpers, guides or witnesses that the group wants to share the ceremony with.

Moving around the circle or randomly, each person places their object in the centre and shares what they want to release. When this is done have a short break (in silence), sing a song or simply change seats and have a body shake on the way.

Now take turns to select an object from the 'Giveaways' that symbolises a change, a new situation or way of being - a gift full of power and meaning for each person to take home.

Don't be concerned about 'taking on other people's stuff' when choosing their object, as the energy is transmuted in the exchange.

However, you may like to cleanse the object by washing it in the ocean or a river, placing it in moonlight followed by sunlight or passing it through the smoke of a fire or smudge stick.

Finish with some form of dance, celebration or shared meal.

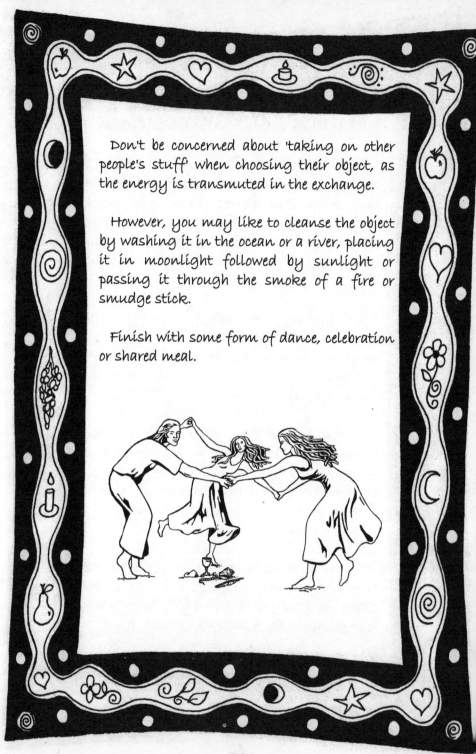

GO
OUT
FOR
DINNER
ALONE

23

GO OUT FOR DINNER ALONE

Invite yourself out for dinner at a special restaurant.

Get all dressed up and take a deep breath. This is a night out just for you.

If you think you'll get bored or lonely take some special things to entertain yourself with. A good book, your journal, an art pad and coloured pens, your knitting!!

Relax and act as if this is a perfectly natural thing to do.

Savour every mouthful of your meal and celebrate this special occasion. Shout yourself a decadent drink. Have two desserts if that's what feels right. Know that you are the perfect dinner companion for yourself.

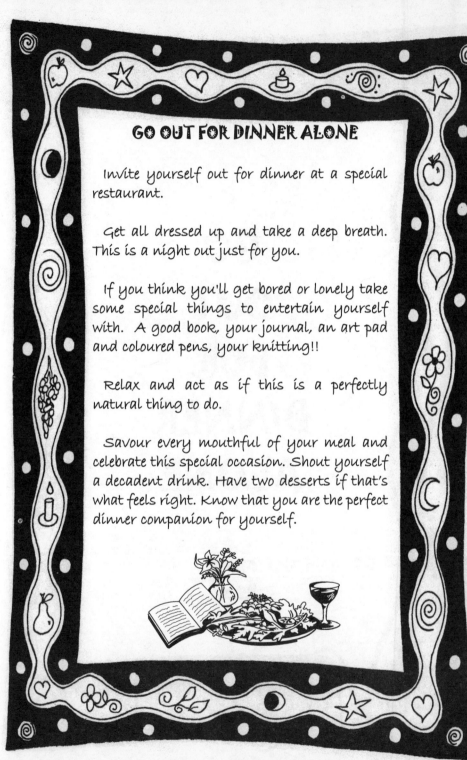

MAKE YOURSELF A HERB TEA

24

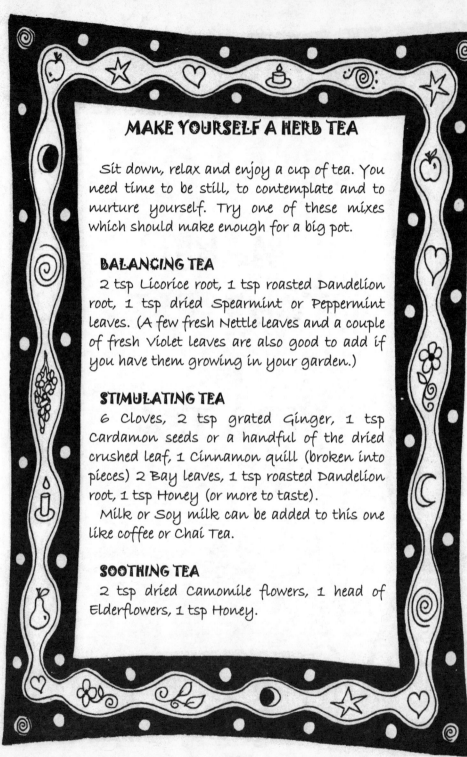

MAKE YOURSELF A HERB TEA

Sit down, relax and enjoy a cup of tea. You need time to be still, to contemplate and to nurture yourself. Try one of these mixes which should make enough for a big pot.

BALANCING TEA
2 tsp Licorice root, 1 tsp roasted Dandelion root, 1 tsp dried Spearmint or Peppermint leaves. (A few fresh Nettle leaves and a couple of fresh Violet leaves are also good to add if you have them growing in your garden.)

STIMULATING TEA
6 Cloves, 2 tsp grated Ginger, 1 tsp Cardamon seeds or a handful of the dried crushed leaf, 1 Cinnamon quill (broken into pieces) 2 Bay leaves, 1 tsp roasted Dandelion root, 1 tsp Honey (or more to taste).
Milk or Soy milk can be added to this one like coffee or Chai Tea.

SOOTHING TEA
2 tsp dried Camomile flowers, 1 head of Elderflowers, 1 tsp Honey.

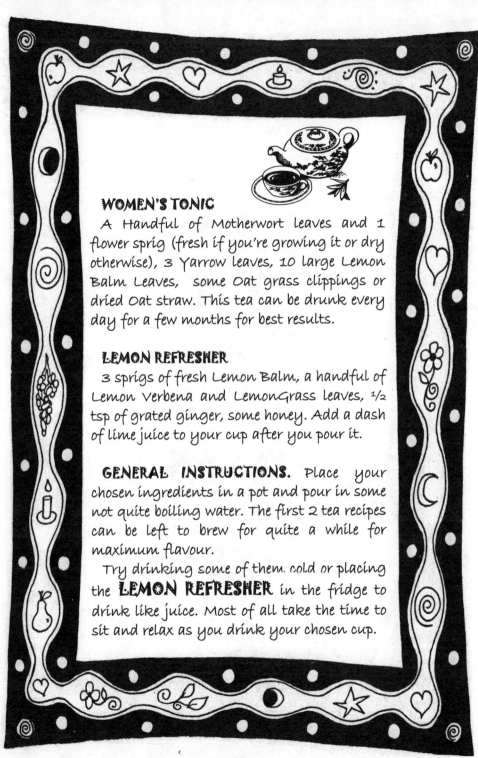

WOMEN'S TONIC

A Handful of Motherwort leaves and 1 flower sprig (fresh if you're growing it or dry otherwise), 3 Yarrow leaves, 10 large Lemon Balm Leaves, some Oat grass clippings or dried Oat straw. This tea can be drunk every day for a few months for best results.

LEMON REFRESHER

3 sprigs of fresh Lemon Balm, a handful of Lemon Verbena and LemonGrass leaves, ½ tsp of grated ginger, some honey. Add a dash of lime juice to your cup after you pour it.

GENERAL INSTRUCTIONS. Place your

chosen ingredients in a pot and pour in some not quite boiling water. The first 2 tea recipes can be left to brew for quite a while for maximum flavour.

Try drinking some of them cold or placing the **LEMON REFRESHER** in the fridge to drink like juice. Most of all take the time to sit and relax as you drink your chosen cup.

GO
FOR
A
LONG
WALK

<u>25</u>

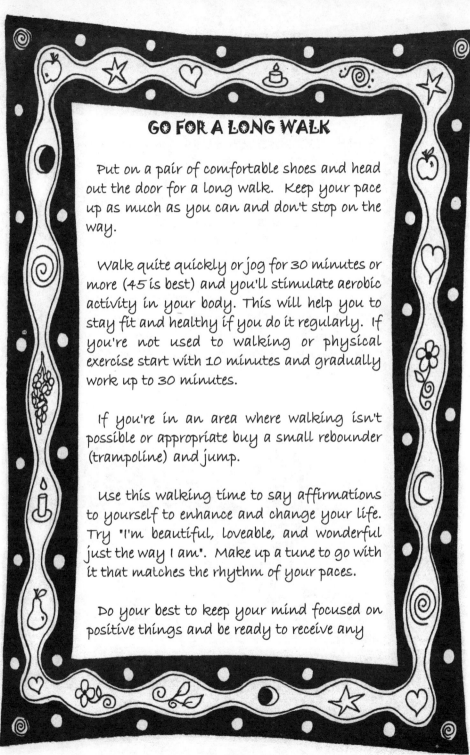

GO FOR A LONG WALK

Put on a pair of comfortable shoes and head out the door for a long walk. Keep your pace up as much as you can and don't stop on the way.

Walk quite quickly or jog for 30 minutes or more (45 is best) and you'll stimulate aerobic activity in your body. This will help you to stay fit and healthy if you do it regularly. If you're not used to walking or physical exercise start with 10 minutes and gradually work up to 30 minutes.

If you're in an area where walking isn't possible or appropriate buy a small rebounder (trampoline) and jump.

Use this walking time to say affirmations to yourself to enhance and change your life. Try "I'm beautiful, loveable, and wonderful just the way I am". Make up a tune to go with it that matches the rhythm of your paces.

Do your best to keep your mind focused on positive things and be ready to receive any little insights that pop up as you relax more and more with each step. If you are jumping on a trampoline keep your breathing in time with the bounces and let each out breath release more tension and unwanted energy from your body, and as someone once said "Let each inbreath be an inspiration".

Make this a daily ritual (or at least 4 times a week) and walk as fast as you can for optimum health and aerobic benefit. Feel the difference this gift makes to your life after 2 or 3 weeks.

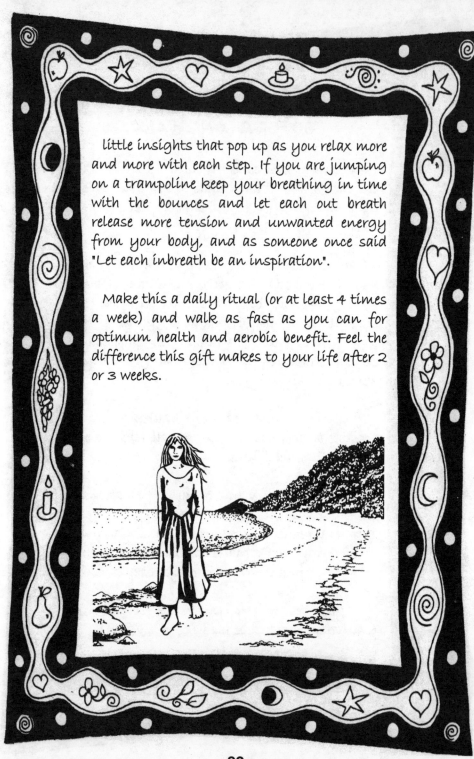

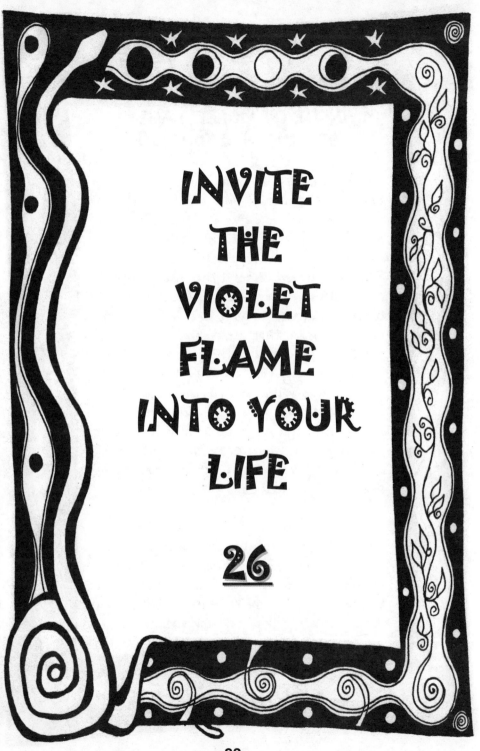

INVITE
THE
VIOLET
FLAME
INTO YOUR
LIFE

26

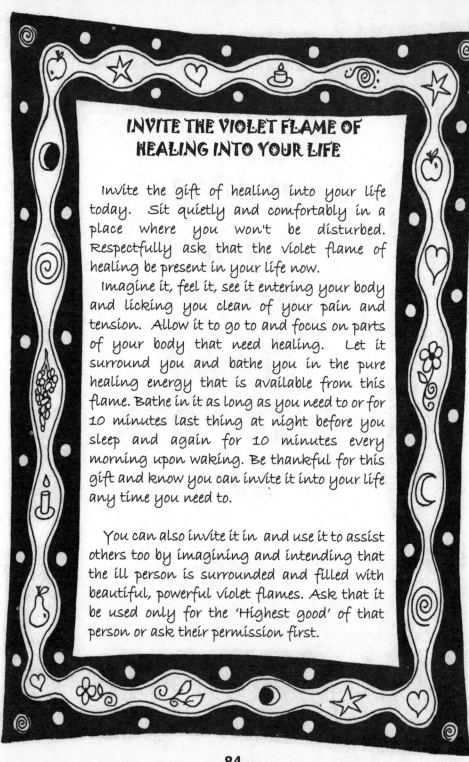

INVITE THE VIOLET FLAME OF HEALING INTO YOUR LIFE

Invite the gift of healing into your life today. Sit quietly and comfortably in a place where you won't be disturbed. Respectfully ask that the violet flame of healing be present in your life now.

Imagine it, feel it, see it entering your body and licking you clean of your pain and tension. Allow it to go to and focus on parts of your body that need healing. Let it surround you and bathe you in the pure healing energy that is available from this flame. Bathe in it as long as you need to or for 10 minutes last thing at night before you sleep and again for 10 minutes every morning upon waking. Be thankful for this gift and know you can invite it into your life any time you need to.

You can also invite it in and use it to assist others too by imagining and intending that the ill person is surrounded and filled with beautiful, powerful violet flames. Ask that it be used only for the 'Highest good' of that person or ask their permission first.

CREATE
A
NEW
GARDEN

27

CREATE A NEW GARDEN

Design and make a new garden where you're living. Get your hands into the soil. Create it magically and with the intent to connect more strongly with Earth.

Plant herbs, flowers, pebbles, crystals and precious stones, leafy greens and other vegetables. Plant lots of harmony and love as you go. All these things are important elements for your new garden.

If you don't have space or aren't in a situation to have a garden, make a miniature one in a pot. Find a ceramic garden planter with saucer or decorate an old plastic pot, the bigger the better.

Plant two or three different plants and whatever else feels appropriate from the things previously mentioned.

When you've finished sit back and take a deep breath. Feel yourself more strongly connected to Earth and to the plants that you've given a new home to.

Treat them like babies, talk to them, encourage them, love and nurture them and as you do so, know that you also give these gifts to yourself.

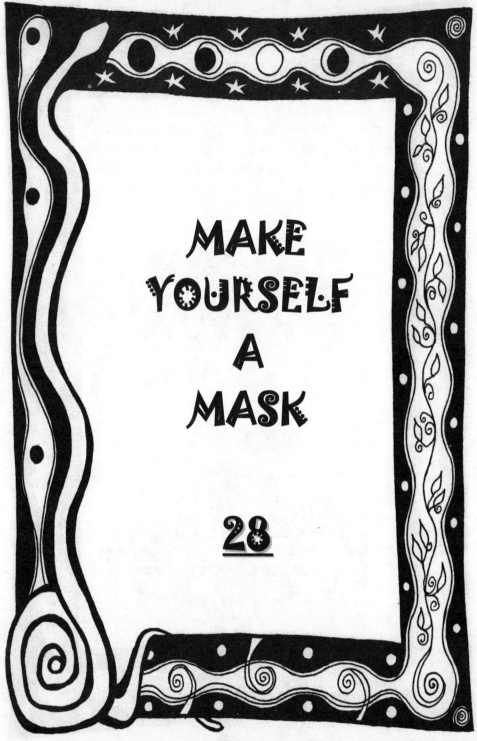

MAKE YOURSELF A MASK

28

MAKE YOURSELF A MASK

Make a mask of your most flamboyant self. What colour is it? Does it have feathers, sequins, glitter, ribbons, bark, moss, leaves? Is it painted with patterns and symbols? Maybe it's a collage. Is it human, does it resemble an animal or is it spacey and abstract?

See if you can 'tune in' to what is right for you. Close your eyes and let a picture come, then go about making it.

Once you've finished, feel the strength, courage and creativity it took to bring this part of yourself to the surface. Invite friends to come and join you and share in this creative process. Wear your mask out at the slightest opportunity or better still create a reason to wear it.

GIVE
FOR
GIVINGS
SAKE

29

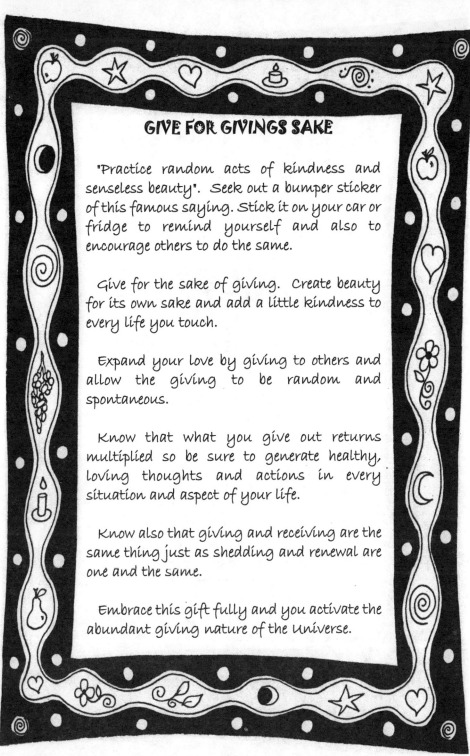

GIVE FOR GIVINGS SAKE

"Practice random acts of kindness and senseless beauty". Seek out a bumper sticker of this famous saying. Stick it on your car or fridge to remind yourself and also to encourage others to do the same.

Give for the sake of giving. Create beauty for its own sake and add a little kindness to every life you touch.

Expand your love by giving to others and allow the giving to be random and spontaneous.

Know that what you give out returns multiplied so be sure to generate healthy, loving thoughts and actions in every situation and aspect of your life.

Know also that giving and receiving are the same thing just as shedding and renewal are one and the same.

Embrace this gift fully and you activate the abundant giving nature of the Universe.

HAVE
A
SWIM

30

HAVE A SWIM

Take the time to go to the ocean or to a flowing stream or river in a natural surrounding. Immerse yourself in the water, naked if possible. Relax. Feel all your tension being rinsed away by the water or swept aside by the waves.

Imagine that you are a rock in the stream, cleansed and caressed by the moving water or imagine that you are a dolphin, frolicking and free in the waves. Spend at least half to one hour visualising, feeling and play-acting this.

Let the sun and the breeze dry your body and give thanks for your renewed freshness and vitality.

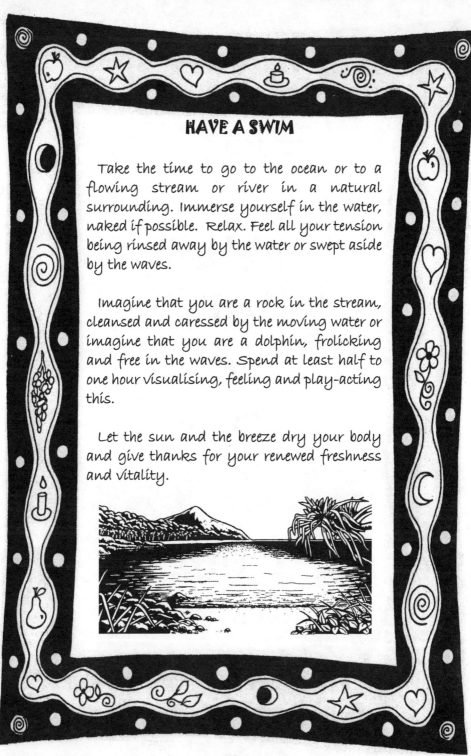

MAKE UP A SONG

31

MAKE UP A SONG

Make up a song to help you through this time in your life.

Think about what's happening for you now. Close your eyes and ask your higher self for the words that you most need to be telling yourself at the moment and then have a go at working this statement up into a tune. Even if it is only one or two lines it will have power for you. Sing it to yourself as often as you can. Dare to sing it out loud.

Driving alone in the car or while you're out walking is an ideal opportunity to use this musical gift which you can give to yourself on a regular basis.

SURRENDER TO THE UNIVERSE

32

SURRENDER TO THE UNIVERSE

What are you holding on to at the moment? What attachment is restricting you in your life? What is the major 'problem' you are experiencing?

Prepare to go on a visualised journey up a mountain taking with you something you want to let go of or release to the Universe for guidance and clarity. (it may be a person, idea, land, problem, desire, question, issue....)

Take a few minutes to relax then begin to see yourself walking out from where you are, along a path which flows and winds its way through familiar territory into the unfamiliar where you begin to walk up a mountain, gradually at first, around bends, past a lake, up, up, until you reach the final ascent up to the top. Make the ascent slowly and gradually. Maybe stop for a rest at a special place along the way. Take a deep breath and look around.

There are clouds clustered around the summit and a soft grassy place to sit and

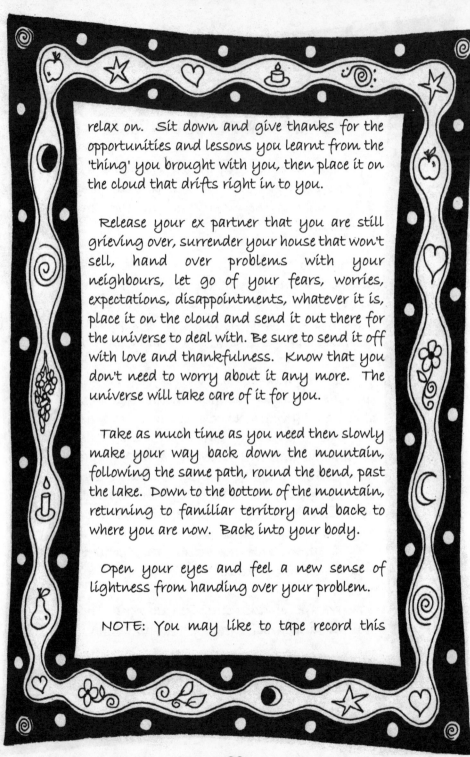

relax on. Sit down and give thanks for the opportunities and lessons you learnt from the 'thing' you brought with you, then place it on the cloud that drifts right in to you.

Release your ex partner that you are still grieving over, surrender your house that won't sell, hand over problems with your neighbours, let go of your fears, worries, expectations, disappointments, whatever it is, place it on the cloud and send it out there for the universe to deal with. Be sure to send it off with love and thankfulness. Know that you don't need to worry about it any more. The universe will take care of it for you.

Take as much time as you need then slowly make your way back down the mountain, following the same path, round the bend, past the lake. Down to the bottom of the mountain, returning to familiar territory and back to where you are now. Back into your body.

Open your eyes and feel a new sense of lightness from handing over your problem.

NOTE: You may like to tape record this

journey or have a friend read it to you.
Embellish it as much as you like. Maybe
imagine yourself taking a cleansing swim
in the lake on the way back down. Which ever
way you do it take it slowly and allow time
for each step in the journey.

I can't emphasise too much how important it
is to return slowly, the same way that you
went up to ensure you are fully back in your
body before you wiggle your fingers, toes,
stretch, yawn and then gently open your
eyes.

GIVE
THANKS
FOR
YOUR
FOOD

33

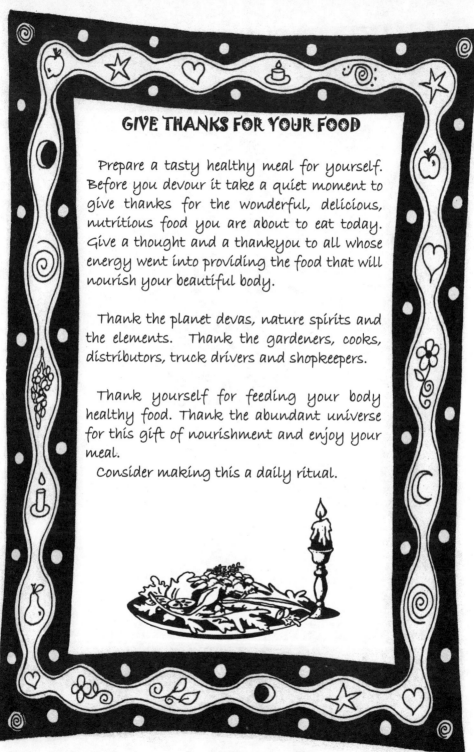

GIVE THANKS FOR YOUR FOOD

Prepare a tasty healthy meal for yourself. Before you devour it take a quiet moment to give thanks for the wonderful, delicious, nutritious food you are about to eat today. Give a thought and a thankyou to all whose energy went into providing the food that will nourish your beautiful body.

Thank the planet devas, nature spirits and the elements. Thank the gardeners, cooks, distributors, truck drivers and shopkeepers.

Thank yourself for feeding your body healthy food. Thank the abundant universe for this gift of nourishment and enjoy your meal.

Consider making this a daily ritual.

CHANGE YOUR HAIR

34

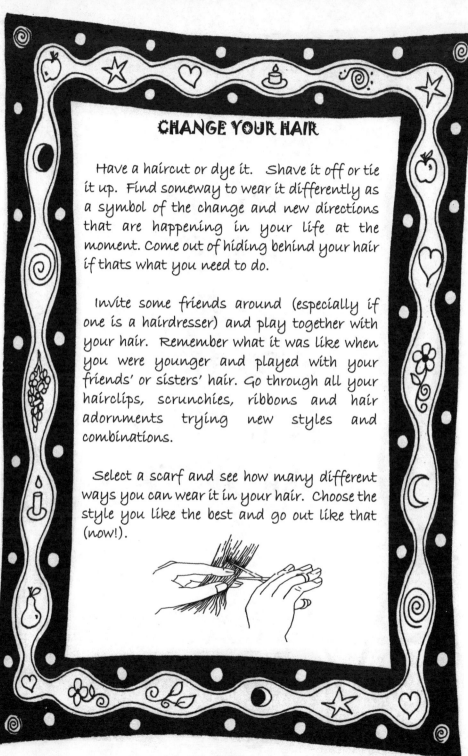

CHANGE YOUR HAIR

Have a haircut or dye it. Shave it off or tie it up. Find someway to wear it differently as a symbol of the change and new directions that are happening in your life at the moment. Come out of hiding behind your hair if thats what you need to do.

Invite some friends around (especially if one is a hairdresser) and play together with your hair. Remember what it was like when you were younger and played with your friends' or sisters' hair. Go through all your hairclips, scrunchies, ribbons and hair adornments trying new styles and combinations.

Select a scarf and see how many different ways you can wear it in your hair. Choose the style you like the best and go out like that (now!).

WRITE A LIST OF TOOLS FOR YOUR GROWTH

35

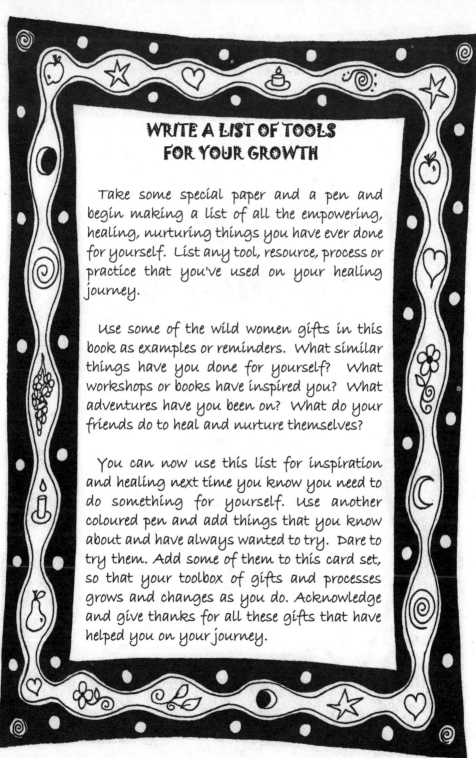

WRITE A LIST OF TOOLS
FOR YOUR GROWTH

Take some special paper and a pen and begin making a list of all the empowering, healing, nurturing things you have ever done for yourself. List any tool, resource, process or practice that you've used on your healing journey.

Use some of the wild women gifts in this book as examples or reminders. What similar things have you done for yourself? What workshops or books have inspired you? What adventures have you been on? What do your friends do to heal and nurture themselves?

You can now use this list for inspiration and healing next time you know you need to do something for yourself. Use another coloured pen and add things that you know about and have always wanted to try. Dare to try them. Add some of them to this card set, so that your toolbox of gifts and processes grows and changes as you do. Acknowledge and give thanks for all these gifts that have helped you on your journey.

ASK
SOMEONE
FOR
A
HUG

36

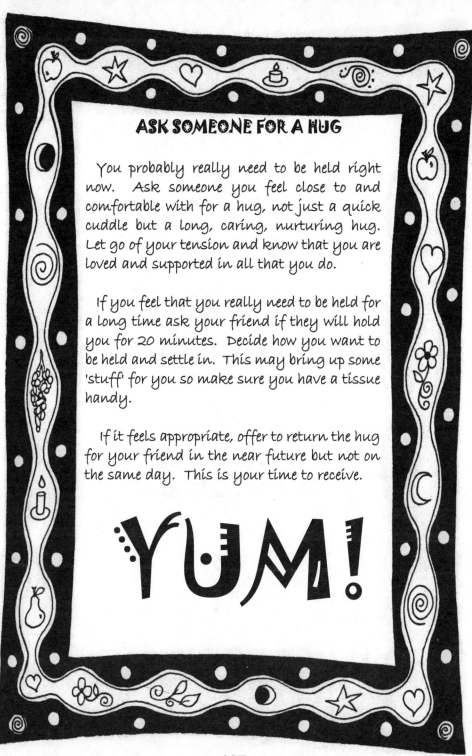

ASK SOMEONE FOR A HUG

You probably really need to be held right now. Ask someone you feel close to and comfortable with for a hug, not just a quick cuddle but a long, caring, nurturing hug. Let go of your tension and know that you are loved and supported in all that you do.

If you feel that you really need to be held for a long time ask your friend if they will hold you for 20 minutes. Decide how you want to be held and settle in. This may bring up some 'stuff' for you so make sure you have a tissue handy.

If it feels appropriate, offer to return the hug for your friend in the near future but not on the same day. This is your time to receive.

YUM!

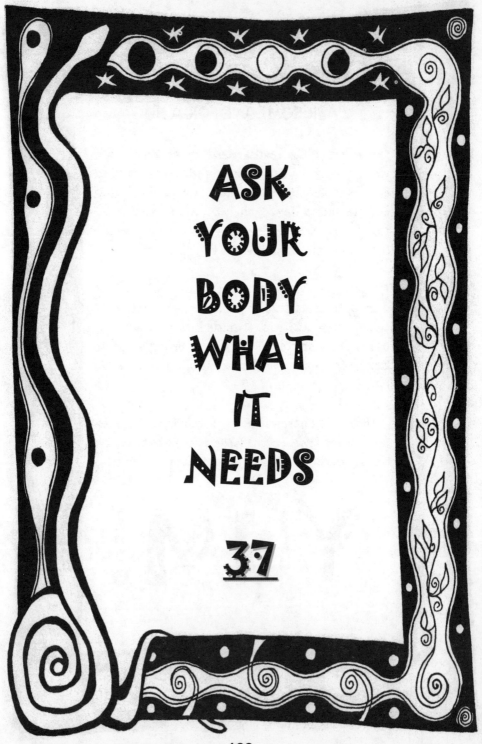

ASK
YOUR
BODY
WHAT
IT
NEEDS

3·7

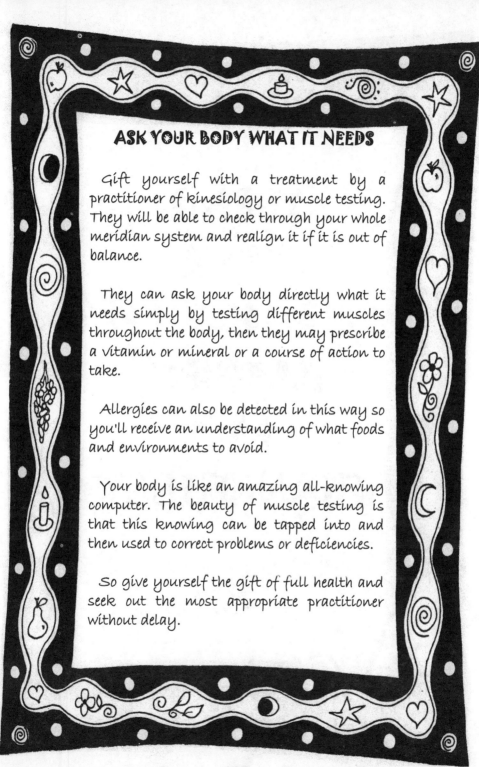

ASK YOUR BODY WHAT IT NEEDS

Gift yourself with a treatment by a practitioner of kinesiology or muscle testing. They will be able to check through your whole meridian system and realign it if it is out of balance.

They can ask your body directly what it needs simply by testing different muscles throughout the body, then they may prescribe a vitamin or mineral or a course of action to take.

Allergies can also be detected in this way so you'll receive an understanding of what foods and environments to avoid.

Your body is like an amazing all-knowing computer. The beauty of muscle testing is that this knowing can be tapped into and then used to correct problems or deficiencies.

So give yourself the gift of full health and seek out the most appropriate practitioner without delay.

SPEND
YOUR
$'s
HAPPILY
AND
THANKFULLY

38

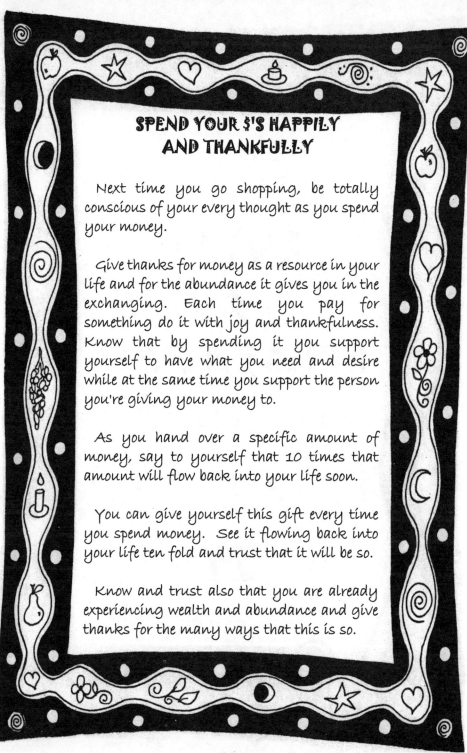

SPEND YOUR $'S HAPPILY AND THANKFULLY

Next time you go shopping, be totally conscious of your every thought as you spend your money.

Give thanks for money as a resource in your life and for the abundance it gives you in the exchanging. Each time you pay for something do it with joy and thankfulness. Know that by spending it you support yourself to have what you need and desire while at the same time you support the person you're giving your money to.

As you hand over a specific amount of money, say to yourself that 10 times that amount will flow back into your life soon.

You can give yourself this gift every time you spend money. See it flowing back into your life ten fold and trust that it will be so.

Know and trust also that you are already experiencing wealth and abundance and give thanks for the many ways that this is so.

ENJOY
A
RELAXATION
EXERCISE

39

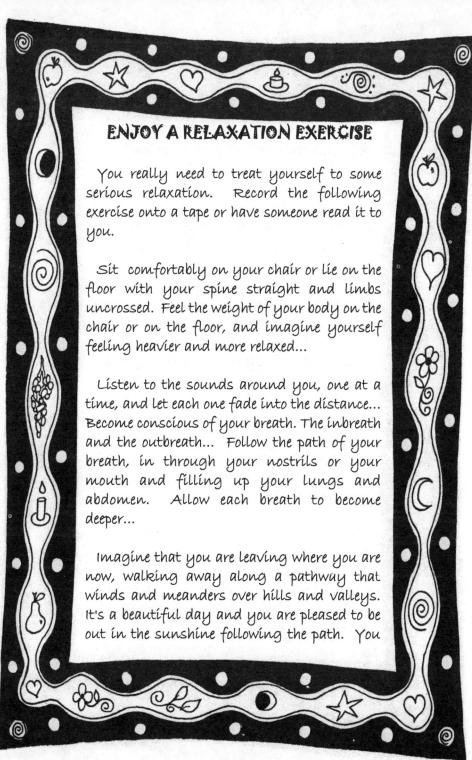

ENJOY A RELAXATION EXERCISE

You really need to treat yourself to some serious relaxation. Record the following exercise onto a tape or have someone read it to you.

Sit comfortably on your chair or lie on the floor with your spine straight and limbs uncrossed. Feel the weight of your body on the chair or on the floor, and imagine yourself feeling heavier and more relaxed...

Listen to the sounds around you, one at a time, and let each one fade into the distance... Become conscious of your breath. The inbreath and the outbreath... Follow the path of your breath, in through your nostrils or your mouth and filling up your lungs and abdomen. Allow each breath to become deeper...

Imagine that you are leaving where you are now, walking away along a pathway that winds and meanders over hills and valleys. It's a beautiful day and you are pleased to be out in the sunshine following the path. You

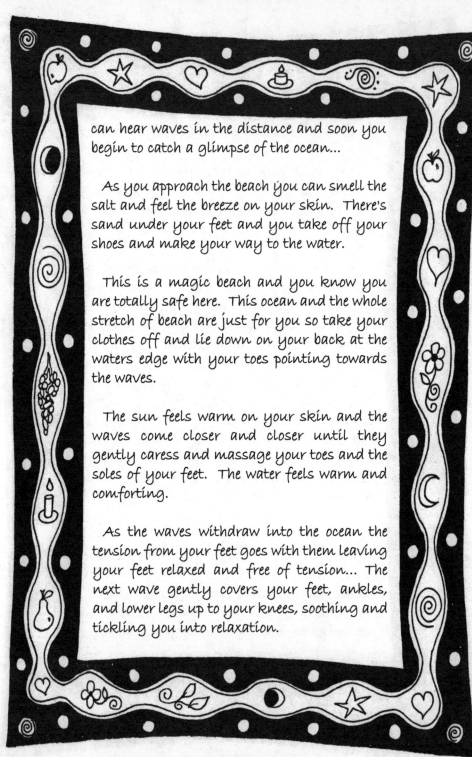

can hear waves in the distance and soon you begin to catch a glimpse of the ocean...

As you approach the beach you can smell the salt and feel the breeze on your skin. There's sand under your feet and you take off your shoes and make your way to the water.

This is a magic beach and you know you are totally safe here. This ocean and the whole stretch of beach are just for you so take your clothes off and lie down on your back at the waters edge with your toes pointing towards the waves.

The sun feels warm on your skin and the waves come closer and closer until they gently caress and massage your toes and the soles of your feet. The water feels warm and comforting.

As the waves withdraw into the ocean the tension from your feet goes with them leaving your feet relaxed and free of tension... The next wave gently covers your feet, ankles, and lower legs up to your knees, soothing and tickling you into relaxation.

The wave retreats, taking tension from your lower legs as it goes... Imagine the waves working through your whole body, right up to the top of your head... Once you've made it this far take a moment to check if there is anywhere in your body still holding tension. use the waves again to release this.

Now make a gradual return to your ordinary consciousness by listening to the sounds around you, becoming conscious again of your breath, stretching and yawning as you "wake up", then opening your eyes. Spend a moment lying on your side before you get up.

Repeat this every day as long as you need to or each night before bed to help you to sleep or to reduce the stress in your life..

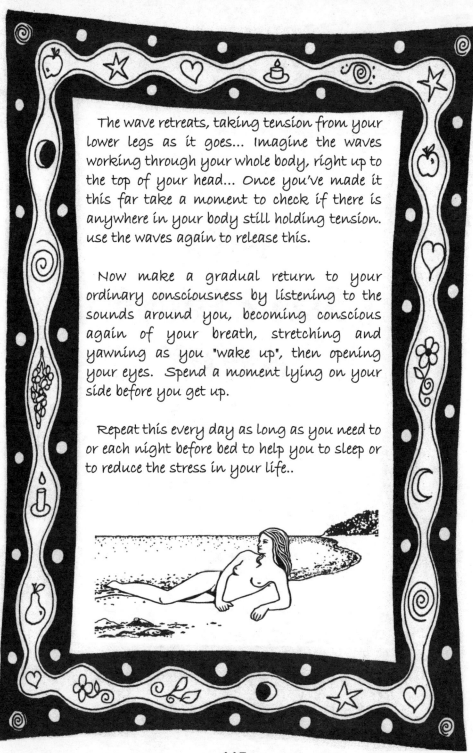

GIVE
SOMETHING
AWAY
TODAY

40

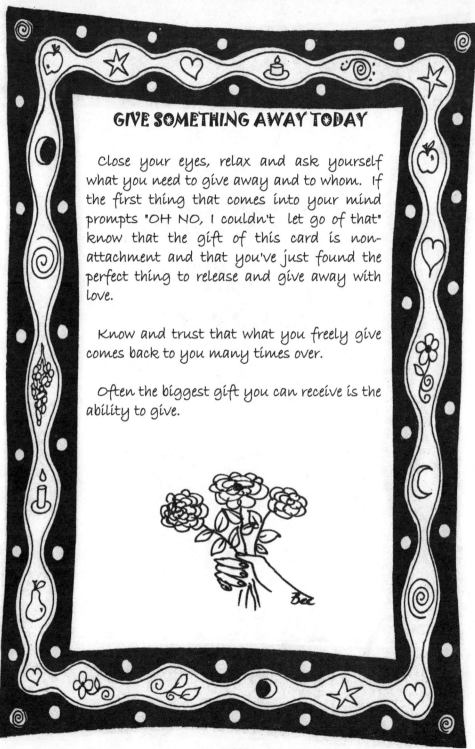

GIVE SOMETHING AWAY TODAY

Close your eyes, relax and ask yourself what you need to give away and to whom. If the first thing that comes into your mind prompts "OH NO, I couldn't let go of that" know that the gift of this card is non-attachment and that you've just found the perfect thing to release and give away with love.

Know and trust that what you freely give comes back to you many times over.

Often the biggest gift you can receive is the ability to give.

CHANGE THE WAY YOU THINK

41

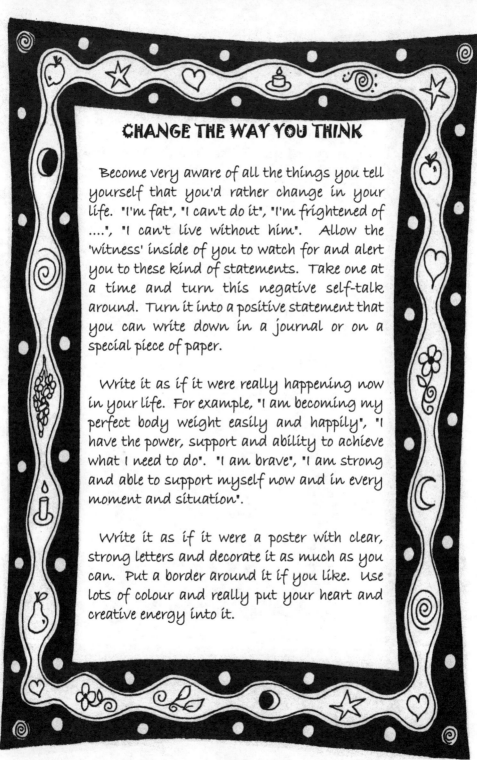

CHANGE THE WAY YOU THINK

Become very aware of all the things you tell yourself that you'd rather change in your life. "I'm fat", "I can't do it", "I'm frightened of ....", "I can't live without him". Allow the 'witness' inside of you to watch for and alert you to these kind of statements. Take one at a time and turn this negative self-talk around. Turn it into a positive statement that you can write down in a journal or on a special piece of paper.

Write it as if it were really happening now in your life. For example, "I am becoming my perfect body weight easily and happily", "I have the power, support and ability to achieve what I need to do". "I am brave", "I am strong and able to support myself now and in every moment and situation".

Write it as if it were a poster with clear, strong letters and decorate it as much as you can. Put a border around it if you like. Use lots of colour and really put your heart and creative energy into it.

You can now pin your affirmation up somewhere so you will see it and read it often, or leave your journal next to the bed for easy access. The best time to say your positive statements is when you first wake up in the morning and as you are going to bed. Read them several times with passion and at the same time visualise yourself really doing it.

Read 'The power is within you' by Louise Hay if you'd like to explore Affirmations more deeply.

MY LIFE FLOWS

INVITE
A
SPECIAL
FRIEND
TO
DINNER

42

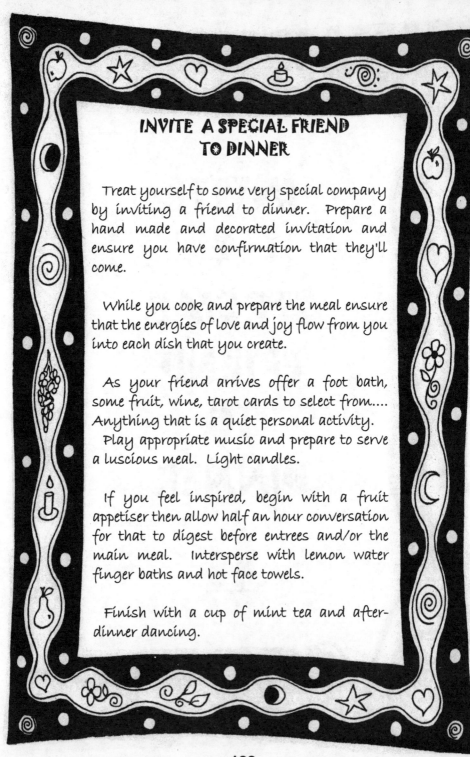

INVITE A SPECIAL FRIEND TO DINNER

Treat yourself to some very special company by inviting a friend to dinner. Prepare a hand made and decorated invitation and ensure you have confirmation that they'll come.

While you cook and prepare the meal ensure that the energies of love and joy flow from you into each dish that you create.

As your friend arrives offer a foot bath, some fruit, wine, tarot cards to select from.... Anything that is a quiet personal activity.

Play appropriate music and prepare to serve a luscious meal. Light candles.

If you feel inspired, begin with a fruit appetiser then allow half an hour conversation for that to digest before entrees and/or the main meal. Intersperse with lemon water finger baths and hot face towels.

Finish with a cup of mint tea and after-dinner dancing.

DO
SOMETHING
YOU'VE
ALWAYS
WANTED
TO DO

43

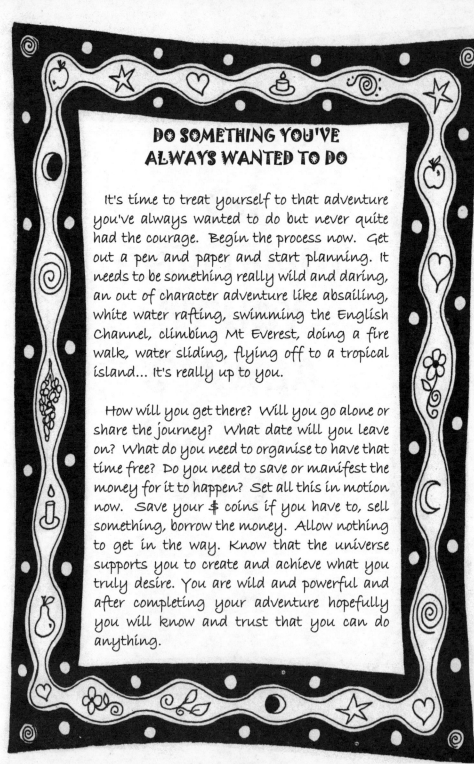

DO SOMETHING YOU'VE ALWAYS WANTED TO DO

It's time to treat yourself to that adventure you've always wanted to do but never quite had the courage. Begin the process now. Get out a pen and paper and start planning. It needs to be something really wild and daring, an out of character adventure like absailing, white water rafting, swimming the English Channel, climbing Mt Everest, doing a fire walk, water sliding, flying off to a tropical island... It's really up to you.

How will you get there? Will you go alone or share the journey? What date will you leave on? What do you need to organise to have that time free? Do you need to save or manifest the money for it to happen? Set all this in motion now. Save your $ coins if you have to, sell something, borrow the money. Allow nothing to get in the way. Know that the universe supports you to create and achieve what you truly desire. You are wild and powerful and after completing your adventure hopefully you will know and trust that you can do anything.

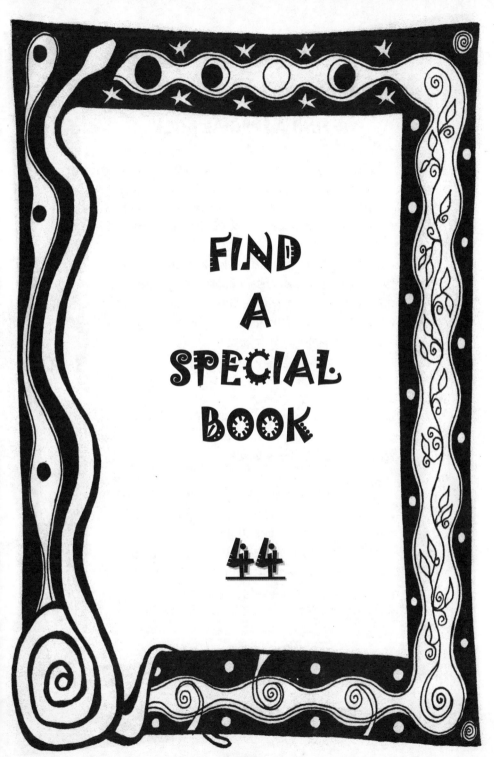

FIND A SPECIAL BOOK

44

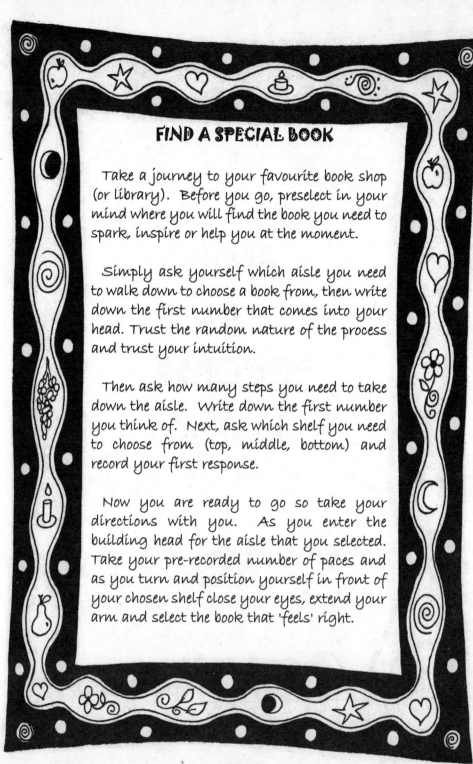

FIND A SPECIAL BOOK

Take a journey to your favourite book shop (or library). Before you go, preselect in your mind where you will find the book you need to spark, inspire or help you at the moment.

Simply ask yourself which aisle you need to walk down to choose a book from, then write down the first number that comes into your head. Trust the random nature of the process and trust your intuition.

Then ask how many steps you need to take down the aisle. Write down the first number you think of. Next, ask which shelf you need to choose from (top, middle, bottom) and record your first response.

Now you are ready to go so take your directions with you. As you enter the building head for the aisle that you selected. Take your pre-recorded number of paces and as you turn and position yourself in front of your chosen shelf close your eyes, extend your arm and select the book that 'feels' right.

Take it home with you knowing and trusting that there is a special message in the book just for you. See if you can work out what that message is.

Ask a specific question about your life and open the book at any page. Survey the information and make associations between what is written and the question you asked. Is there an answer or solution there for you?

IT'S
TIME
TO
CELEBRATE

45

ITS TIME TO CELEBRATE

How long since you've hosted a party? This time invite only your women friends and ask them to come dressed as their most wildest woman. (If it feels really appropriate ask your male friends as well but insist they come dressed as their most wildest woman.)

Decorate your home or chosen venue in an appropriate way and ask everyone to bring food to share for a meal so it doesn't take too much time to organise. Also request each person to bring a wild or unconventional gift valued at under $10 which is gift wrapped. Let all your friends know that the party is for all of you to celebrate being wild women and being friends.

During the event allow time and space for rituals, games, sharing, storytelling or performances. Create a special circle for a ceremony where everyone chooses a gift to take home.

Most of all HAVE FUN while emphasising the wild nature of the event.

DRAW YOURSELF A PICTURE

46

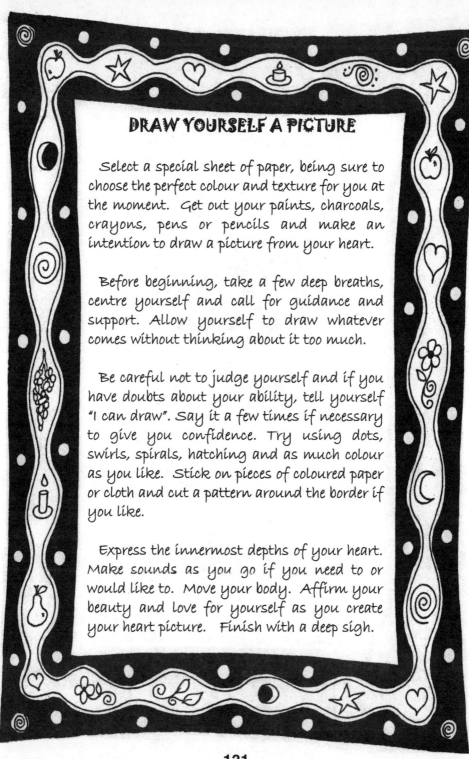

DRAW YOURSELF A PICTURE

Select a special sheet of paper, being sure to choose the perfect colour and texture for you at the moment. Get out your paints, charcoals, crayons, pens or pencils and make an intention to draw a picture from your heart.

Before beginning, take a few deep breaths, centre yourself and call for guidance and support. Allow yourself to draw whatever comes without thinking about it too much.

Be careful not to judge yourself and if you have doubts about your ability, tell yourself "I can draw". Say it a few times if necessary to give you confidence. Try using dots, swirls, spirals, hatching and as much colour as you like. Stick on pieces of coloured paper or cloth and cut a pattern around the border if you like.

Express the innermost depths of your heart. Make sounds as you go if you need to or would like to. Move your body. Affirm your beauty and love for yourself as you create your heart picture. Finish with a deep sigh.

CREATE YOUR DREAM

47

CREATE YOUR DREAM

Write down what you most wish for in your life. Write it as if it is actually happening now. Do you dream of your own home, a trip overseas, a meaningful and fun job or a relationship that is perfect for you? Whatever you dream, see it as clearly as you can in your mind and then write down all the details. Imagine yourself living your dream. What does it feel like to be doing what you've always wanted? Write all this down as well. The feelings, the support you envisage you need, the colours, sounds and smells. The more you can bring to life your picture and recording of your dream the better.

After you've finished, read it aloud to yourself and really feel that you are living your dream. Make a commitment to yourself to read this every day. Remember to imagine yourself doing it as you read and change it, add details and adjust it to suit your growing vision, day by day.

Know that you have the power to live your dreams.

INTRODUCE
TITHING
INTO
YOUR
LIFE

48

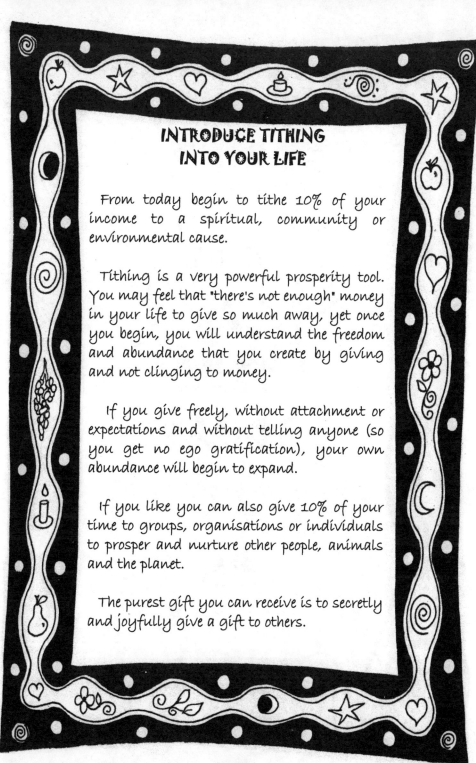

INTRODUCE TITHING INTO YOUR LIFE

From today begin to tithe 10% of your income to a spiritual, community or environmental cause.

Tithing is a very powerful prosperity tool. You may feel that "there's not enough" money in your life to give so much away, yet once you begin, you will understand the freedom and abundance that you create by giving and not clinging to money.

If you give freely, without attachment or expectations and without telling anyone (so you get no ego gratification), your own abundance will begin to expand.

If you like you can also give 10% of your time to groups, organisations or individuals to prosper and nurture other people, animals and the planet.

The purest gift you can receive is to secretly and joyfully give a gift to others.

HUG A TREE TODAY

49

HUG A TREE TODAY

Take a walk in a forest, the local park, or your own backyard, looking specifically for a special tree. It can be a tree that you find great beauty in or one that you feel calls you to be with it.

Spend some time being close to the tree, letting your energies blend, then have a hug. Wrap your arms around the tree and feel your heart centre connect with the life energy of this mighty one legged being.

After a while become aware of your breath and begin to feel a cycle of breathing taking place between you and the tree. As you breathe in, sense yourself breathing in the ancient connectedness of the tree. As you breathe out your carbon dioxide is inhaled by the tree. Then as you breath in you in turn inhale the fresh oxygen that tree has just exuded.

For at least 10 minutes continue this cycle of breathing, the two of you exchanging oxygen and carbon dioxide. Feel your heart opening and connecting with your new

friend. Know that you are related in a very special way. Contemplate what this means for you.

As you approach the end of your sharing with tree ask if it has a message for you and be open and aware of any thoughts, ideas, impressions or musings you have immediately after you ask this.

Be sure to thank the tree for connecting with you and complete your sharing in any way that feels appropriate.

START
A
HEALING
FUND

50

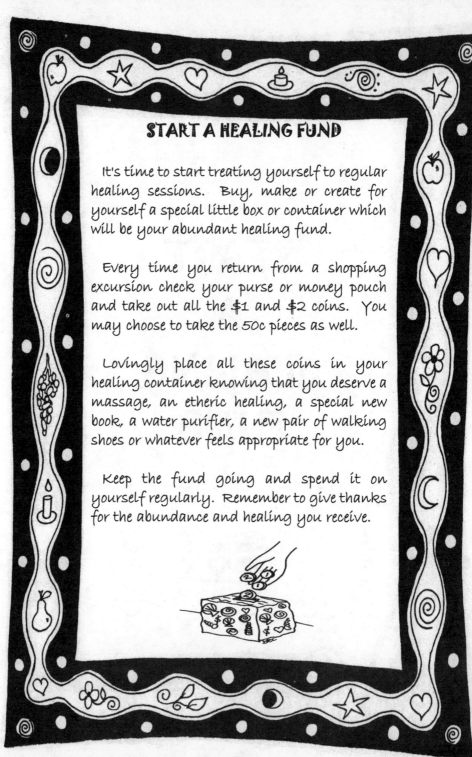

START A HEALING FUND

It's time to start treating yourself to regular healing sessions. Buy, make or create for yourself a special little box or container which will be your abundant healing fund.

Every time you return from a shopping excursion check your purse or money pouch and take out all the $1 and $2 coins. You may choose to take the 50c pieces as well.

Lovingly place all these coins in your healing container knowing that you deserve a massage, an etheric healing, a special new book, a water purifier, a new pair of walking shoes or whatever feels appropriate for you.

Keep the fund going and spend it on yourself regularly. Remember to give thanks for the abundance and healing you receive.

WEED YOUR COSMIC GARDEN

51

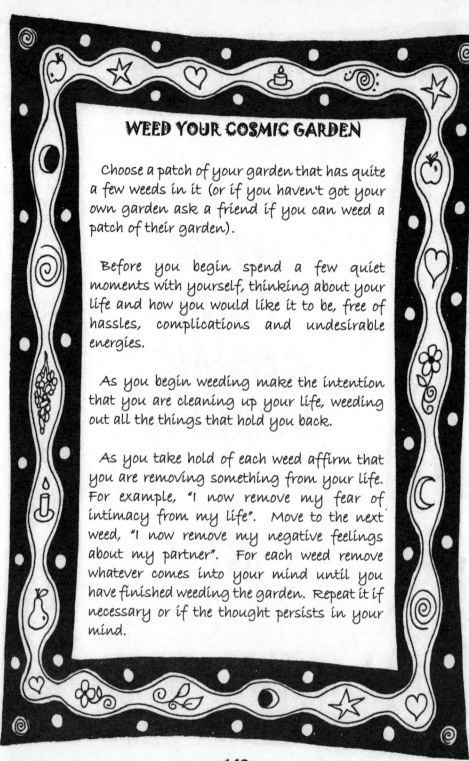

WEED YOUR COSMIC GARDEN

Choose a patch of your garden that has quite a few weeds in it (or if you haven't got your own garden ask a friend if you can weed a patch of their garden).

Before you begin spend a few quiet moments with yourself, thinking about your life and how you would like it to be, free of hassles, complications and undesirable energies.

As you begin weeding make the intention that you are cleaning up your life, weeding out all the things that hold you back.

As you take hold of each weed affirm that you are removing something from your life. For example, "I now remove my fear of intimacy from my life". Move to the next weed, "I now remove my negative feelings about my partner". For each weed remove whatever comes into your mind until you have finished weeding the garden. Repeat it if necessary or if the thought persists in your mind.

When you are finished make a pile of all the weeds and create a little ritual where you sprinkle the pile with your good intentions (lime, liquid manure or rock minerals could all be symbolic of this). Declare that you now transform all the weeds into rich organic matter which will feed and nourish the garden (and your spirit) in the future.

You could complete the process by mulching the garden while affirming that you are feeding and giving to yourself things like warmth, protection, nourishment and strength. Plant new plants if there are gaps in your newly weeded garden. As you plant each one also plant hope, trust, joy, peace and bliss. Water in the new plants with love.

VISIT
A
SACRED
SITE

52

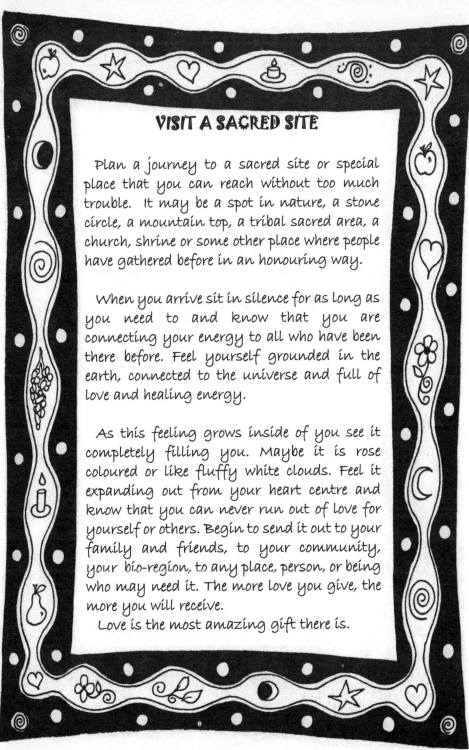

VISIT A SACRED SITE

Plan a journey to a sacred site or special place that you can reach without too much trouble. It may be a spot in nature, a stone circle, a mountain top, a tribal sacred area, a church, shrine or some other place where people have gathered before in an honouring way.

When you arrive sit in silence for as long as you need to and know that you are connecting your energy to all who have been there before. Feel yourself grounded in the earth, connected to the universe and full of love and healing energy.

As this feeling grows inside of you see it completely filling you. Maybe it is rose coloured or like fluffy white clouds. Feel it expanding out from your heart centre and know that you can never run out of love for yourself or others. Begin to send it out to your family and friends, to your community, your bio-region, to any place, person, or being who may need it. The more love you give, the more you will receive.

Love is the most amazing gift there is.

WRITE
YOURSELF
A
LETTER

53

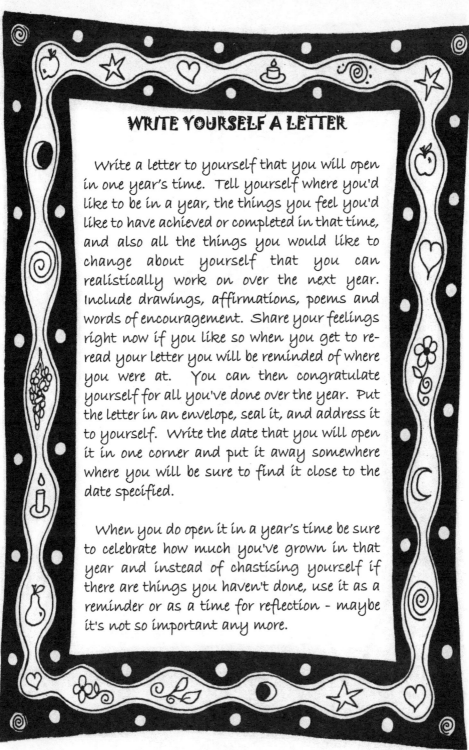

WRITE YOURSELF A LETTER

Write a letter to yourself that you will open in one year's time. Tell yourself where you'd like to be in a year, the things you feel you'd like to have achieved or completed in that time, and also all the things you would like to change about yourself that you can realistically work on over the next year. Include drawings, affirmations, poems and words of encouragement. Share your feelings right now if you like so when you get to re-read your letter you will be reminded of where you were at. You can then congratulate yourself for all you've done over the year. Put the letter in an envelope, seal it, and address it to yourself. Write the date that you will open it in one corner and put it away somewhere where you will be sure to find it close to the date specified.

When you do open it in a year's time be sure to celebrate how much you've grown in that year and instead of chastising yourself if there are things you haven't done, use it as a reminder or as a time for reflection - maybe it's not so important any more.

HAVE A MASSAGE

54

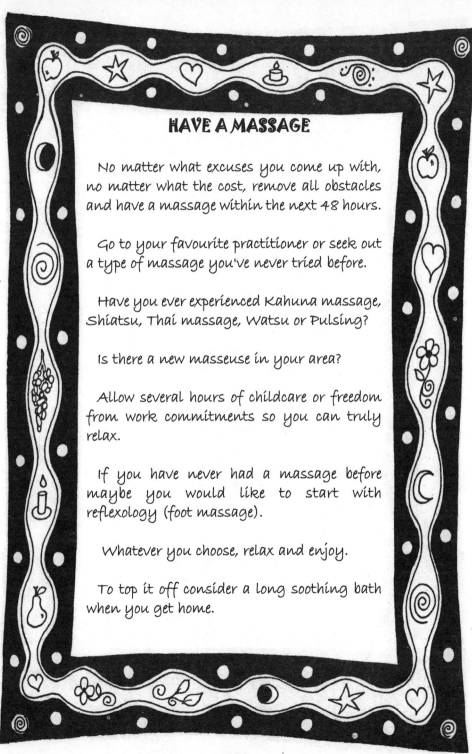

HAVE A MASSAGE

No matter what excuses you come up with, no matter what the cost, remove all obstacles and have a massage within the next 48 hours.

Go to your favourite practitioner or seek out a type of massage you've never tried before.

Have you ever experienced Kahuna massage, Shiatsu, Thai massage, Watsu or Pulsing?

Is there a new masseuse in your area?

Allow several hours of childcare or freedom from work commitments so you can truly relax.

If you have never had a massage before maybe you would like to start with reflexology (foot massage).

Whatever you choose, relax and enjoy.

To top it off consider a long soothing bath when you get home.

ADD
MORE
ALIVENESS
TO
YOUR
LIFE

55

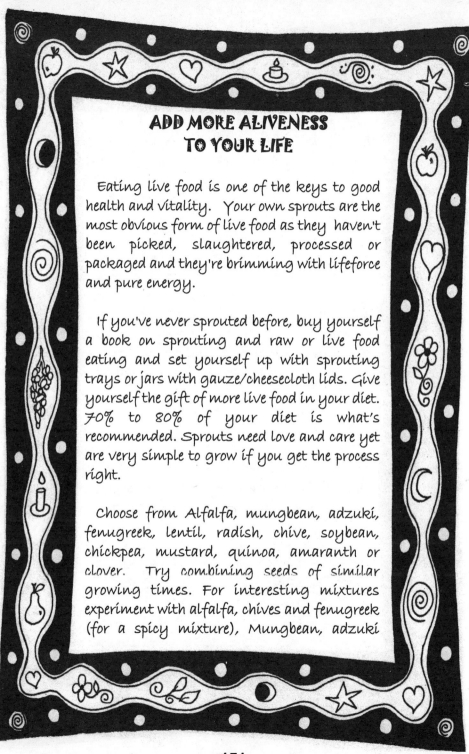

ADD MORE ALIVENESS
TO YOUR LIFE

Eating live food is one of the keys to good health and vitality. Your own sprouts are the most obvious form of live food as they haven't been picked, slaughtered, processed or packaged and they're brimming with lifeforce and pure energy.

If you've never sprouted before, buy yourself a book on sprouting and raw or live food eating and set yourself up with sprouting trays or jars with gauze/cheesecloth lids. Give yourself the gift of more live food in your diet. 70% to 80% of your diet is what's recommended. Sprouts need love and care yet are very simple to grow if you get the process right.

Choose from Alfalfa, mungbean, adzuki, fenugreek, lentil, radish, chive, soybean, chickpea, mustard, quinoa, amaranth or clover. Try combining seeds of similar growing times. For interesting mixtures experiment with alfalfa, chives and fenugreek (for a spicy mixture), Mungbean, adzuki and lentil (for a hearty salad mix). Quinoa and clover . If the weather is humid alfalfa, soybean and chickpea can rot so stick to the other seeds in really warm weather. Mungbean and lentil seem to grow all year round.

Experiment with growing 'clipping' sprouts in trays of soil or special garden beds close to the house for easy cutting to throw into a salad at the last minute. Seeds to experiment with are buckwheat, pea, snowpea, sunflower and mustard. Barley and wheat can be grown like this for their grass which you can chew, juice or add to salads and sandwiches when young. Cut when they're 6cm to 10cm high.

Alfalfa can also be grown like this; the 15cm clippings blended with water and honey then strained for a powerful health tonic.
        Drink and eat to your good health.

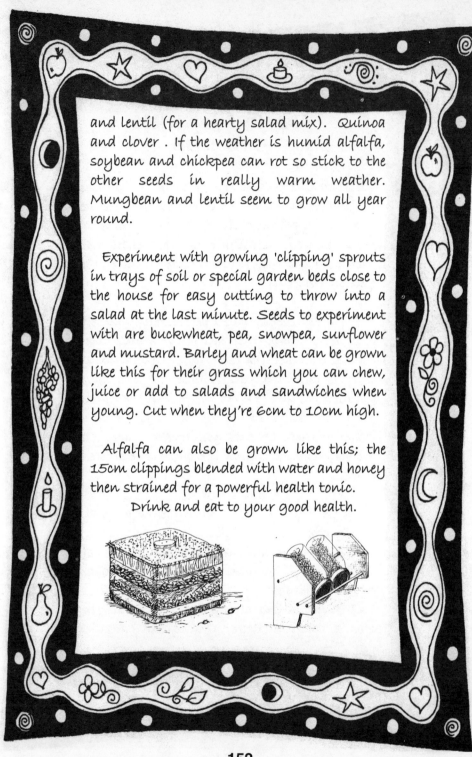

HEAL
AN
OLD
WOUND

56

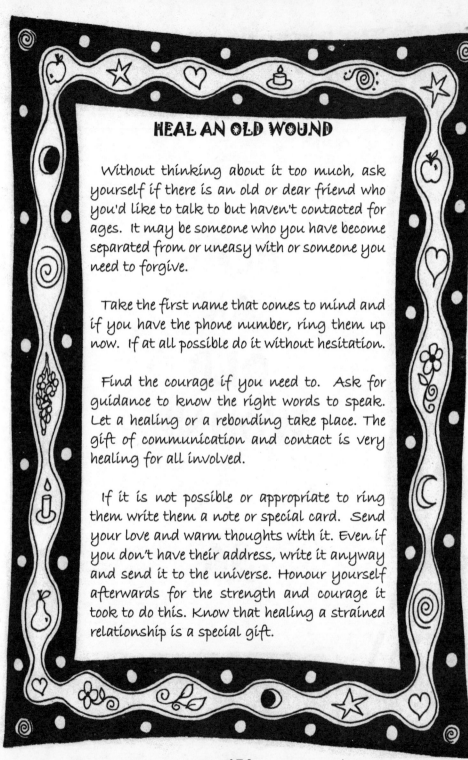

HEAL AN OLD WOUND

Without thinking about it too much, ask yourself if there is an old or dear friend who you'd like to talk to but haven't contacted for ages. It may be someone who you have become separated from or uneasy with or someone you need to forgive.

Take the first name that comes to mind and if you have the phone number, ring them up now. If at all possible do it without hesitation.

Find the courage if you need to. Ask for guidance to know the right words to speak. Let a healing or a rebonding take place. The gift of communication and contact is very healing for all involved.

If it is not possible or appropriate to ring them write them a note or special card. Send your love and warm thoughts with it. Even if you don't have their address, write it anyway and send it to the universe. Honour yourself afterwards for the strength and courage it took to do this. Know that healing a strained relationship is a special gift.

LIE
ON
THE
EARTH

57

LIE ON THE EARTH

Take some time to ground yourself fully.

Spend ten to twenty minutes lying on the earth. If at all possible, go to a forest close by. The back lawn will do though and if you don't have one, try your neighbour's' lawn or a sheltered place in your local park.

If you can find some leaf litter to lie in all the better. Partially cover yourself in leaves. Feel yourself connecting with the ground, with Earth.

Imagine your body is feeling heavier, relaxing, sinking, melting into the warmth and receptivity of earth. Become part of the earth. Grow roots and weave yourself into the soil.

Take a deep, deep breath and totally relax.

Know that you can do this anytime that the big wide world gets too much or if you feel scattered, lightheaded or ungrounded.

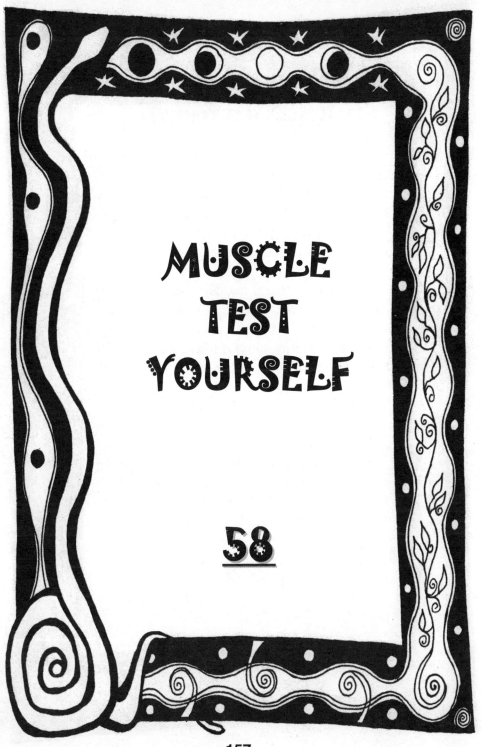

MUSCLE TEST YOURSELF

58

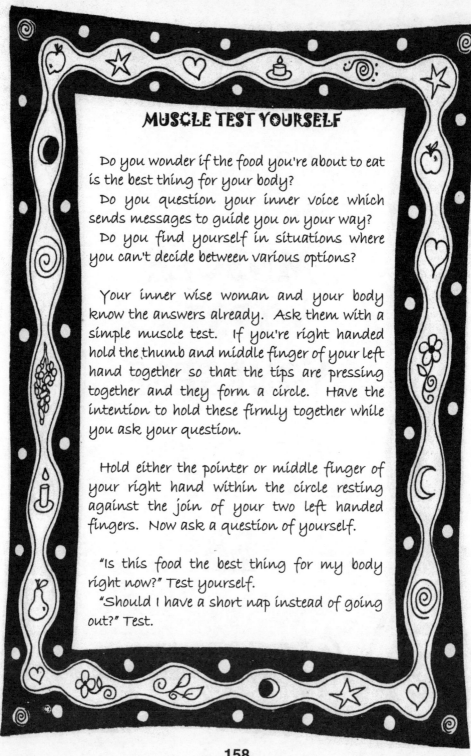

MUSCLE TEST YOURSELF

Do you wonder if the food you're about to eat is the best thing for your body?

Do you question your inner voice which sends messages to guide you on your way?

Do you find yourself in situations where you can't decide between various options?

Your inner wise woman and your body know the answers already. Ask them with a simple muscle test. If you're right handed hold the thumb and middle finger of your left hand together so that the tips are pressing together and they form a circle. Have the intention to hold these firmly together while you ask your question.

Hold either the pointer or middle finger of your right hand within the circle resting against the join of your two left handed fingers. Now ask a question of yourself.

"Is this food the best thing for my body right now?" Test yourself.

"Should I have a short nap instead of going out?" Test.

"Is the grief I'm feeling at the moment mine?" (sometimes we 'pick up' other peoples feelings, thoughts, judgements). "Do I really need to be feeling this/worrying about this at the moment?"

As you ask your question do your best to hold the left hand fingers together while the right hand finger pushes against the join trying to push through and away from the circle. If the circle holds and is strong you have a clear yes. If the circle breaks and your right hand finger comes flying through you have a very clear no. If the circle is weak and starts to part, you have a no that is not so strong.

Once you become comfortable with using this test you will have a valuable tool, a special gift that connects you directly to your divine truth and inner knowing. Be conscious not to place any neediness or weight on the question. Ask it without attachment to the outcome. Pose the question a few times in different ways if you need to check the result. For left handed people, reverse hands.

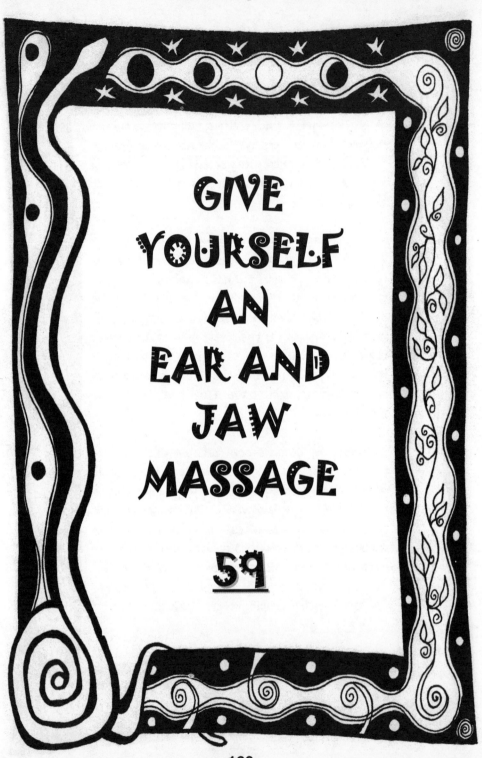

GIVE YOURSELF AN EAR AND JAW MASSAGE

59

GIVE YOURSELF AN
EAR AND JAW MASSAGE

Take a few moments to wake up and 'switch on' your brain and hearing abilities, This is especially helpful if you're about to listen to a long talk or lecture or needing to focus on lots of auditory information.

Reach up and hold the tip of your ears with your thumb and forefingers. Begin to work down the ear rolling out the curl, pulling and stretching out the ear until you pull gently down on the lobe. Repeat this as many times as you like.

Now move to the point where your jaw hinges and begin massaging (we hold lots of tension here), move your jaw up and down and allow yourself to yawn freely. The yawning is important as this helps send additional oxygen to the brain while the ear massage balances and activates our hearing and listening abilities.

Swap an ear massage with a friend for optimum sensation and relaxation.

BUY A SET OF JUGGLING BALLS

60

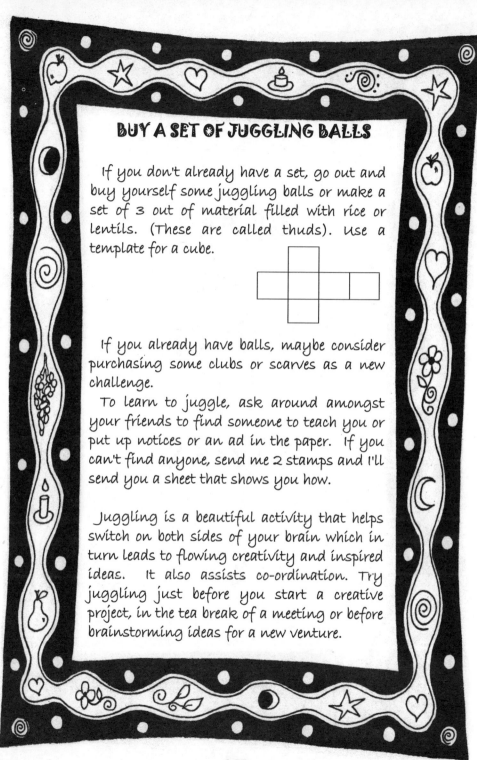

BUY A SET OF JUGGLING BALLS

If you don't already have a set, go out and buy yourself some juggling balls or make a set of 3 out of material filled with rice or lentils. (These are called thuds). Use a template for a cube.

If you already have balls, maybe consider purchasing some clubs or scarves as a new challenge.

To learn to juggle, ask around amongst your friends to find someone to teach you or put up notices or an ad in the paper. If you can't find anyone, send me 2 stamps and I'll send you a sheet that shows you how.

Juggling is a beautiful activity that helps switch on both sides of your brain which in turn leads to flowing creativity and inspired ideas. It also assists co-ordination. Try juggling just before you start a creative project, in the tea break of a meeting or before brainstorming ideas for a new venture.

SLEEP OUT UNDER THE STARS

61

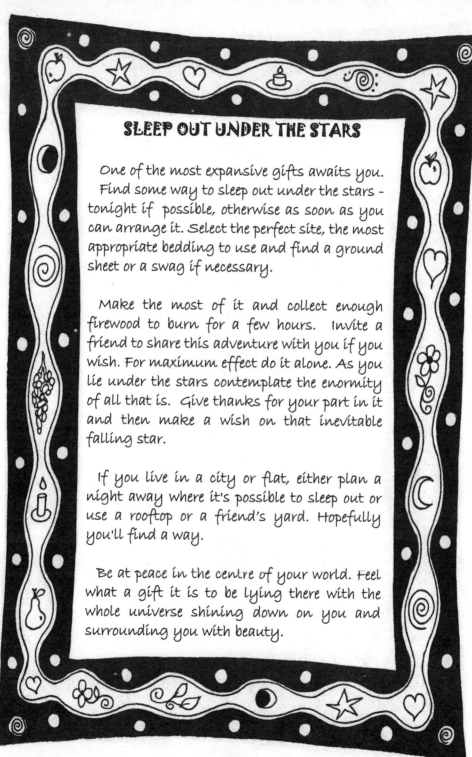

SLEEP OUT UNDER THE STARS

One of the most expansive gifts awaits you. Find some way to sleep out under the stars - tonight if possible, otherwise as soon as you can arrange it. Select the perfect site, the most appropriate bedding to use and find a ground sheet or a swag if necessary.

Make the most of it and collect enough firewood to burn for a few hours. Invite a friend to share this adventure with you if you wish. For maximum effect do it alone. As you lie under the stars contemplate the enormity of all that is. Give thanks for your part in it and then make a wish on that inevitable falling star.

If you live in a city or flat, either plan a night away where it's possible to sleep out or use a rooftop or a friend's yard. Hopefully you'll find a way.

Be at peace in the centre of your world. Feel what a gift it is to be lying there with the whole universe shining down on you and surrounding you with beauty.

UNDERTAKE A 'VISION QUEST'

62

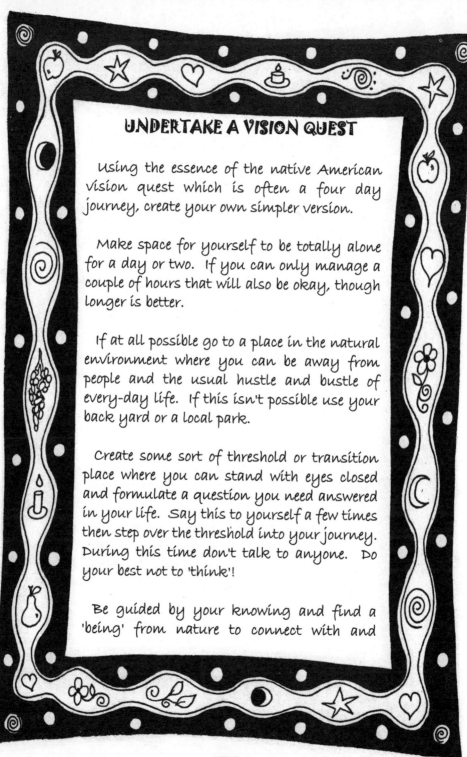

UNDERTAKE A VISION QUEST

Using the essence of the native American vision quest which is often a four day journey, create your own simpler version.

Make space for yourself to be totally alone for a day or two. If you can only manage a couple of hours that will also be okay, though longer is better.

If at all possible go to a place in the natural environment where you can be away from people and the usual hustle and bustle of every-day life. If this isn't possible use your back yard or a local park.

Create some sort of threshold or transition place where you can stand with eyes closed and formulate a question you need answered in your life. Say this to yourself a few times then step over the threshold into your journey. During this time don't talk to anyone. Do your best not to 'think'!

Be guided by your knowing and find a 'being' from nature to connect with and

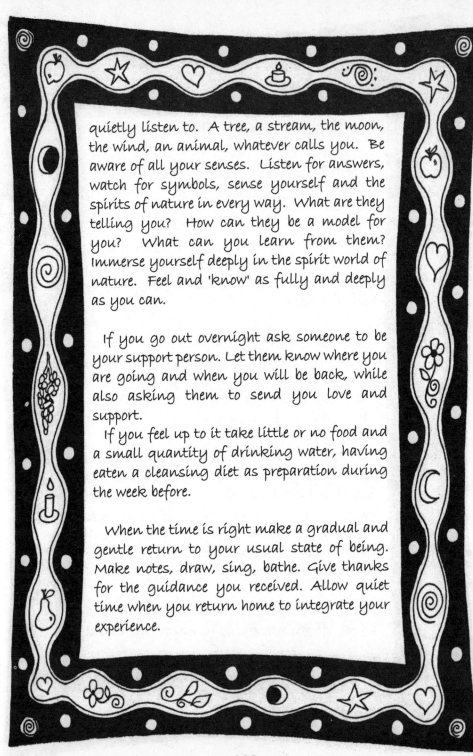

quietly listen to. A tree, a stream, the moon, the wind, an animal, whatever calls you. Be aware of all your senses. Listen for answers, watch for symbols, sense yourself and the spirits of nature in every way. What are they telling you? How can they be a model for you? What can you learn from them? Immerse yourself deeply in the spirit world of nature. Feel and 'know' as fully and deeply as you can.

If you go out overnight ask someone to be your support person. Let them know where you are going and when you will be back, while also asking them to send you love and support.

If you feel up to it take little or no food and a small quantity of drinking water, having eaten a cleansing diet as preparation during the week before.

When the time is right make a gradual and gentle return to your usual state of being. Make notes, draw, sing, bathe. Give thanks for the guidance you received. Allow quiet time when you return home to integrate your experience.

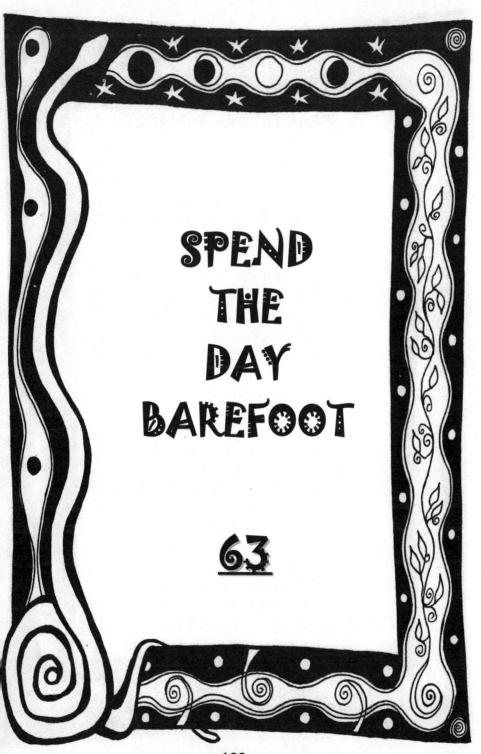

SPEND
THE
DAY
BAREFOOT

63

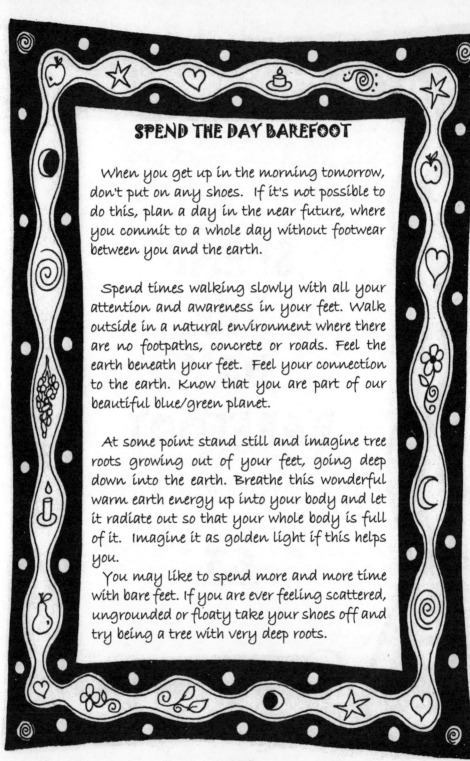

SPEND THE DAY BAREFOOT

When you get up in the morning tomorrow, don't put on any shoes. If it's not possible to do this, plan a day in the near future, where you commit to a whole day without footwear between you and the earth.

Spend times walking slowly with all your attention and awareness in your feet. Walk outside in a natural environment where there are no footpaths, concrete or roads. Feel the earth beneath your feet. Feel your connection to the earth. Know that you are part of our beautiful blue/green planet.

At some point stand still and imagine tree roots growing out of your feet, going deep down into the earth. Breathe this wonderful warm earth energy up into your body and let it radiate out so that your whole body is full of it. Imagine it as golden light if this helps you.

You may like to spend more and more time with bare feet. If you are ever feeling scattered, ungrounded or floaty take your shoes off and try being a tree with very deep roots.

DRESS AS A WILD WOMAN

64

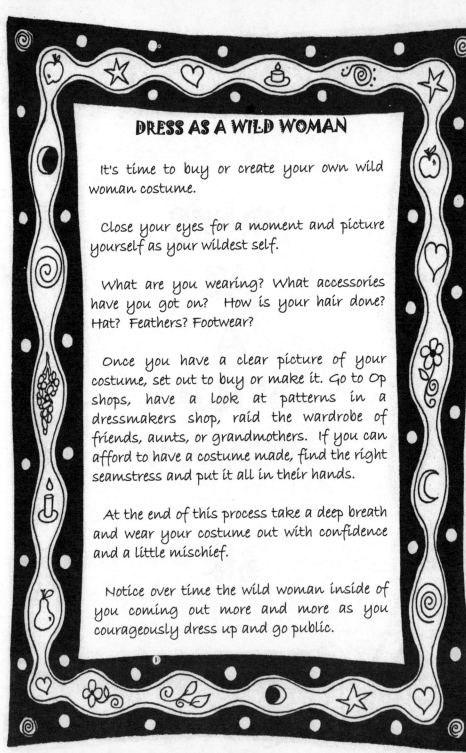

DRESS AS A WILD WOMAN

It's time to buy or create your own wild woman costume.

Close your eyes for a moment and picture yourself as your wildest self.

What are you wearing? What accessories have you got on? How is your hair done? Hat? Feathers? Footwear?

Once you have a clear picture of your costume, set out to buy or make it. Go to Op shops, have a look at patterns in a dressmakers shop, raid the wardrobe of friends, aunts, or grandmothers. If you can afford to have a costume made, find the right seamstress and put it all in their hands.

At the end of this process take a deep breath and wear your costume out with confidence and a little mischief.

Notice over time the wild woman inside of you coming out more and more as you courageously dress up and go public.

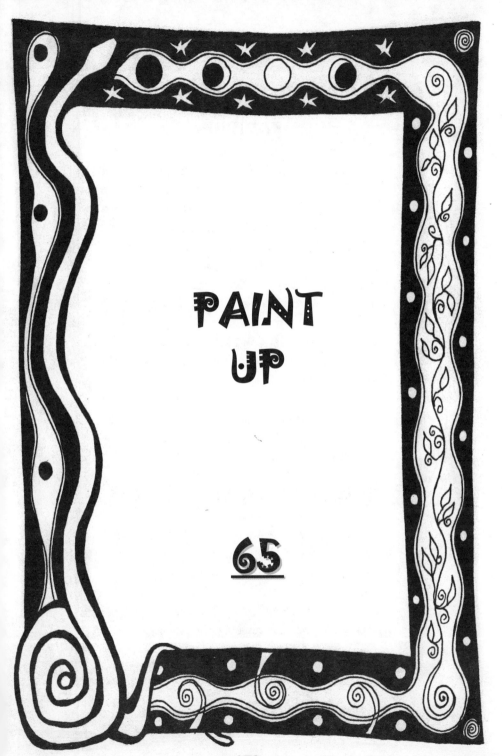

PAINT UP

65

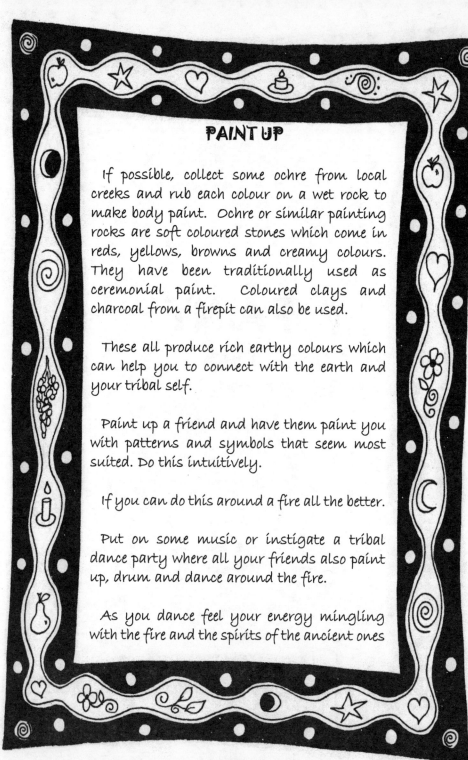

PAINT UP

If possible, collect some ochre from local creeks and rub each colour on a wet rock to make body paint. Ochre or similar painting rocks are soft coloured stones which come in reds, yellows, browns and creamy colours. They have been traditionally used as ceremonial paint. Coloured clays and charcoal from a firepit can also be used.

These all produce rich earthy colours which can help you to connect with the earth and your tribal self.

Paint up a friend and have them paint you with patterns and symbols that seem most suited. Do this intuitively.

If you can do this around a fire all the better.

Put on some music or instigate a tribal dance party where all your friends also paint up, drum and dance around the fire.

As you dance feel your energy mingling with the fire and the spirits of the ancient ones of the earth. Know that their energy will pulse through you if you invite them in.

If you're not able to access painting stones try using face paint or acrylic art paint yet restrict yourself to rich earthy colours.

FILL
YOUR
HEART
WITH
LOVE

66

FILL YOUR HEART WITH LOVE

Sit quietly in a special place and connect into your source energy in any way that works for you.

Feel the pure energy of the universe flowing in through the top of your head, flowing down your arms, your body and filling up your whole being right down to the tip of your toes. Feel the peace and lightness of this energy inside of you. Become aware of your heart and feel it full with this energy as well, With each inbreath feel your heart expand until it seems like it is the size of your whole chest.

Continue to expand your heart energy with each in-breath, and then on every out-breath send some of it out to people who you know need it, to troubled spots around the world, to those who you don't see eye to eye with.

Imagine your love and heart energy creeping out from you to fill your house, local town, suburb, city, state, gradually filling your country, expanding more and more until it covers the whole globe.

After completing this process be aware that you will probably be quite expanded as well. See your energy coming back into your own body and place your hands over your heart for as long as you need to. Allow some time alone before mixing with people again.

While you're in this quiet space gather yourself some scissors and sheets of coloured paper or cardboard (red, pink, purple and green preferably). While the love in your heart is still strong begin cutting out large hearts. Stick them all around your home, office or wherever is appropriate as a continual reminder of the love you feel inside.

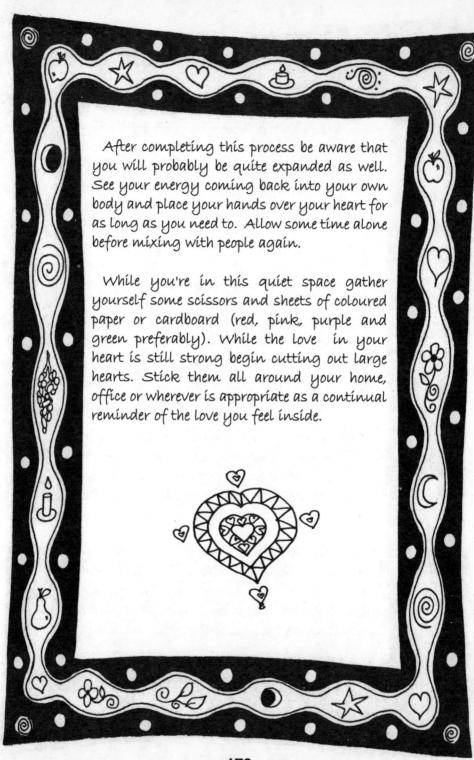

ASK
FOR
HELP

67

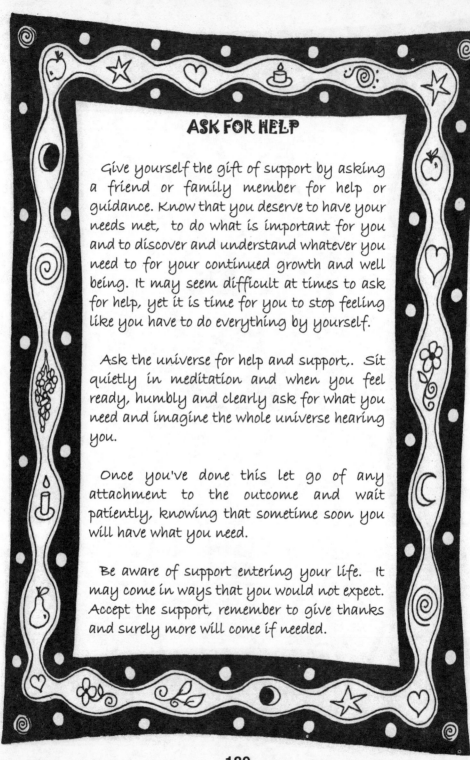

ASK FOR HELP

Give yourself the gift of support by asking a friend or family member for help or guidance. Know that you deserve to have your needs met, to do what is important for you and to discover and understand whatever you need to for your continued growth and well being. It may seem difficult at times to ask for help, yet it is time for you to stop feeling like you have to do everything by yourself.

Ask the universe for help and support,. Sit quietly in meditation and when you feel ready, humbly and clearly ask for what you need and imagine the whole universe hearing you.

Once you've done this let go of any attachment to the outcome and wait patiently, knowing that sometime soon you will have what you need.

Be aware of support entering your life. It may come in ways that you would not expect. Accept the support, remember to give thanks and surely more will come if needed.

TRUST
YOURSELF

68

TRUST YOURSELF

What a gift it is to truly trust yourself and open up your knowing and intuition!

To begin (or remember) to do this, write a list of deep personal questions that you would dearly like answers to. Ask a friend to be the 'interviewer' and recorder.

Sit in meditation until you become fully relaxed and your mind is clear. At this point indicate to your friend to begin asking the questions slowly and clearly. Speak the first thing that comes into your mind and your friend will record it. Don't worry if it seems a bit odd - speak it anyway. If no response comes directly, your friend can move onto the next question and come back to it later.

Suggest to your friend that they work with their intuition as well and ask you anything else that they feel inspired to.

Use the essence of this process in your daily life anytime you need to clarify something.

Ask yourself a question and take the spontaneous response as the true answer. Trust that answer and act on it.

The more you follow this 'first voice' (which is your subconscious knowing) the more that voice will be there to guide you.

What is the most important thing for me to be doing at the moment?

Should I take this new job or travel overseas?

Who or what can guide me on my path to wholeness?

When is the best time to sell my land? ......

MAKE A CLAY FACE MASK OR BODYSUIT

69

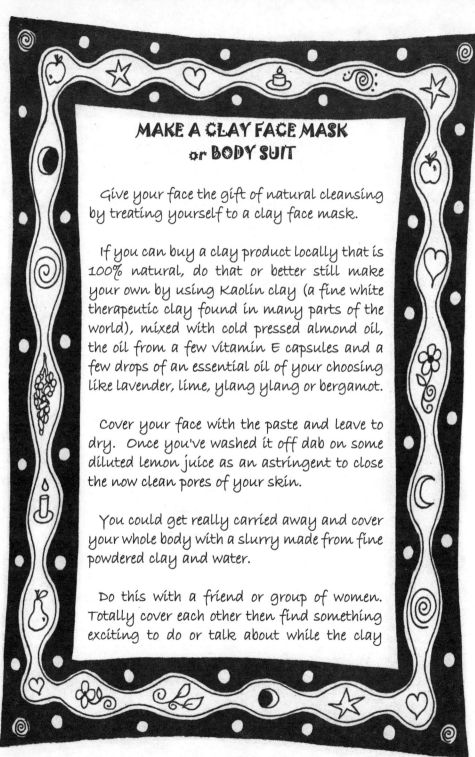

MAKE A CLAY FACE MASK
or BODY SUIT

Give your face the gift of natural cleansing by treating yourself to a clay face mask.

If you can buy a clay product locally that is 100% natural, do that or better still make your own by using Kaolin clay (a fine white therapeutic clay found in many parts of the world), mixed with cold pressed almond oil, the oil from a few vitamin E capsules and a few drops of an essential oil of your choosing like lavender, lime, ylang ylang or bergamot.

Cover your face with the paste and leave to dry. Once you've washed it off dab on some diluted lemon juice as an astringent to close the now clean pores of your skin.

You could get really carried away and cover your whole body with a slurry made from fine powdered clay and water.

Do this with a friend or group of women. Totally cover each other then find something exciting to do or talk about while the clay dries. (It's important to let it dry thoroughly as it is drawing toxins from your body as it dries.)

Wash it all off in a warm shower or ideally in a flowing stream.

Enjoy the gift of a clean refreshed body and sharing this time with friends.

CHANGE YOUR OLD PATTERNS

70

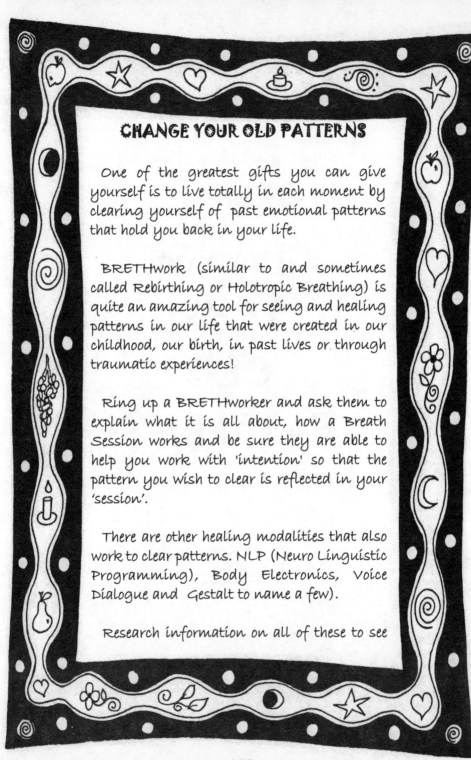

CHANGE YOUR OLD PATTERNS

One of the greatest gifts you can give yourself is to live totally in each moment by clearing yourself of past emotional patterns that hold you back in your life.

BRETHwork (similar to and sometimes called Rebirthing or Holotropic Breathing) is quite an amazing tool for seeing and healing patterns in our life that were created in our childhood, our birth, in past lives or through traumatic experiences!

Ring up a BRETHworker and ask them to explain what it is all about, how a Breath Session works and be sure they are able to help you work with 'intention' so that the pattern you wish to clear is reflected in your 'session'.

There are other healing modalities that also work to clear patterns. NLP (Neuro Linguistic Programming), Body Electronics, Voice Dialogue and Gestalt to name a few).

Research information on all of these to see

which would suit you best.

After doing a few 'sessions' hopefully you will find yourself responding to situations rather that reacting because you've been hurt in a similar way in the past.

What a gift it is to be fully clear and responsive. 'YEH'!

CREATE A SACRED CIRCLE

·71

CREATE A SACRED CIRCLE

Design and plan to build a sacred circle in your own backyard. If this is not possible investigate other options. (Make sure you have full permission first).

▷　Friends places

▷　Local botanical gardens

▷　Scenic sites

▷　National parks or Nature Reserves

▷　Vacant Blocks

Gather rocks that have been sculpted and smoothed by nature and form them into a circle the size that suits your needs. It may be a small circle just big enough for you to sit in or it may be large enough for a whole gathering of people to stand in or around.

If possible place the circle where you can watch the sun and moon rise, or on top of a hill so you can see out in all directions as well.

As you create your circle incorporate gems, special stones and symbols in each of the four directions or anywhere that feels appropriate.

You may like to plant flavouring herbs, shrubs or groundcovers around the outside and create an entrance (traditionally to the East in North American teachings).

Use the space to meditate, give thanks, call in guides and helpers, heal, connect, celebrate or simply to relax in a quiet protected space.

Read up on medicine wheels to explore other ways to use your circle.

START YOUR OWN JOURNAL

72

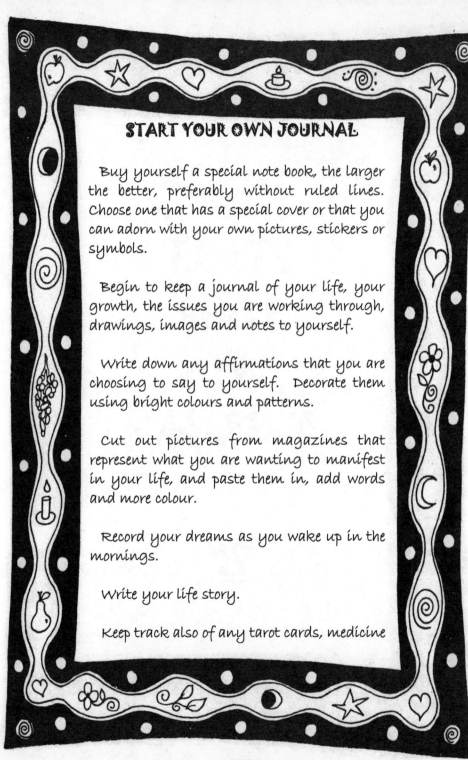

START YOUR OWN JOURNAL

Buy yourself a special note book, the larger the better, preferably without ruled lines. Choose one that has a special cover or that you can adorn with your own pictures, stickers or symbols.

Begin to keep a journal of your life, your growth, the issues you are working through, drawings, images and notes to yourself.

Write down any affirmations that you are choosing to say to yourself. Decorate them using bright colours and patterns.

Cut out pictures from magazines that represent what you are wanting to manifest in your life, and paste them in, add words and more colour.

Record your dreams as you wake up in the mornings.

Write your life story.

Keep track also of any tarot cards, medicine

cards or other divination messages that you have chosen. Record processes and insights, jokes and tribulations. Keep note of any 'wise words' or quotes that ring true for you or that you want to remember.

Use it also to process what is coming up for you at the moment. Write down how you feel and why. Keep writing till you reach a point of clarity and deep understanding. Cry, scream, laugh as you go.

Anytime you need some encouragement or confirmation of how far you've come, go back through your journal. Use it each night and morning to remember to speak your affirmations to yourself.

The most important thing is to use it regularly, over time.

BUY YOURSELF A DIVINATION TOOL

73

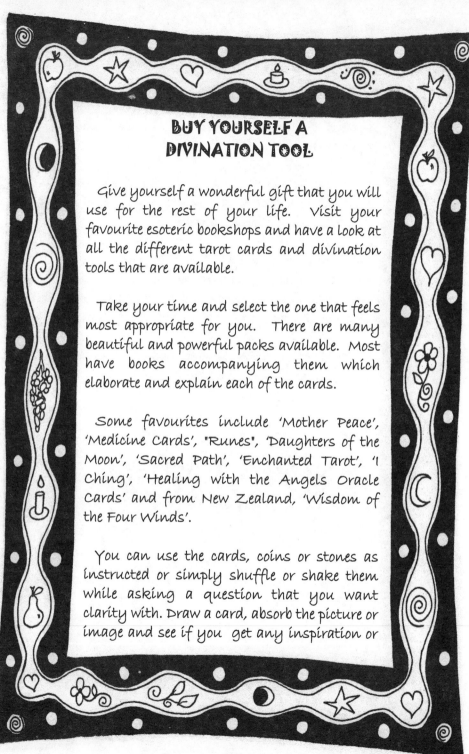

BUY YOURSELF A DIVINATION TOOL

Give yourself a wonderful gift that you will use for the rest of your life. Visit your favourite esoteric bookshops and have a look at all the different tarot cards and divination tools that are available.

Take your time and select the one that feels most appropriate for you. There are many beautiful and powerful packs available. Most have books accompanying them which elaborate and explain each of the cards.

Some favourites include 'Mother Peace', 'Medicine Cards', "Runes", 'Daughters of the Moon', 'Sacred Path', 'Enchanted Tarot', 'I Ching', 'Healing with the Angels Oracle Cards' and from New Zealand, 'Wisdom of the Four Winds'.

You can use the cards, coins or stones as instructed or simply shuffle or shake them while asking a question that you want clarity with. Draw a card, absorb the picture or image and see if you get any inspiration or intuitive guidance before you read the appropriate message in the companion book.

Most importantly, ask only questions for your highest good and you will receive clear, guided and appropriate answers.

It's fine to simply play with them, yet unless the question has real meaning for you, you may not get an answer that has much depth or insight.

Use them in times of deep change or when you need some objective advice or wisdom.

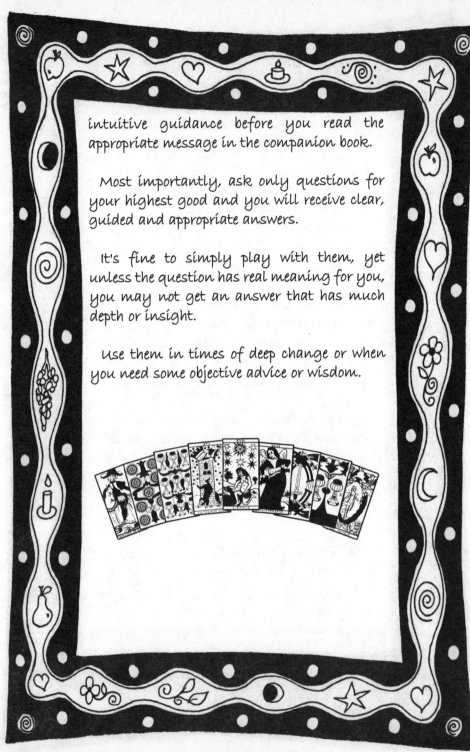

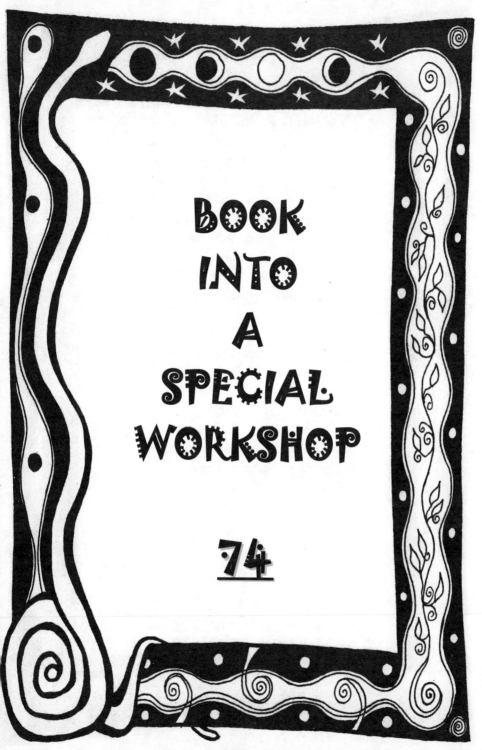

BOOK
INTO
A
SPECIAL
WORKSHOP

74

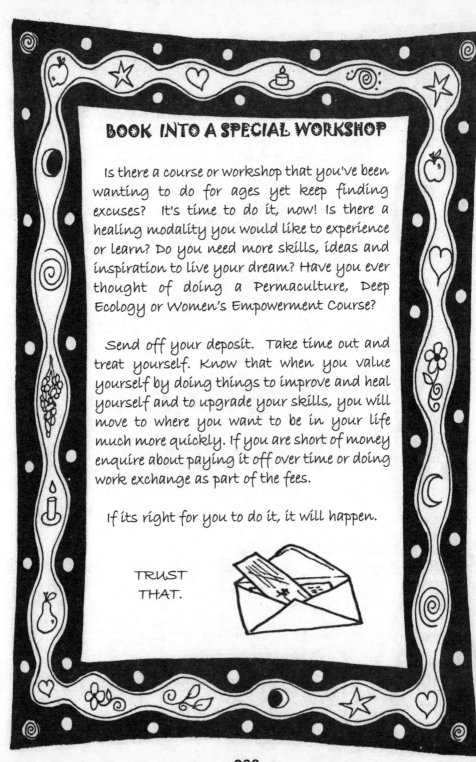

BOOK INTO A SPECIAL WORKSHOP

Is there a course or workshop that you've been wanting to do for ages yet keep finding excuses? It's time to do it, now! Is there a healing modality you would like to experience or learn? Do you need more skills, ideas and inspiration to live your dream? Have you ever thought of doing a Permaculture, Deep Ecology or Women's Empowerment Course?

Send off your deposit. Take time out and treat yourself. Know that when you value yourself by doing things to improve and heal yourself and to upgrade your skills, you will move to where you want to be in your life much more quickly. If you are short of money enquire about paying it off over time or doing work exchange as part of the fees.

If its right for you to do it, it will happen.

TRUST
THAT.

LEARN TO PLAY AN INSTRUMENT

75

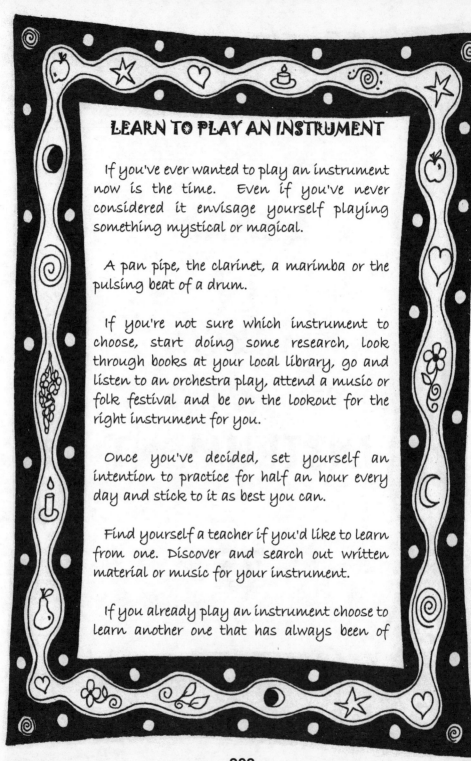

LEARN TO PLAY AN INSTRUMENT

If you've ever wanted to play an instrument now is the time. Even if you've never considered it envisage yourself playing something mystical or magical.

A pan pipe, the clarinet, a marimba or the pulsing beat of a drum.

If you're not sure which instrument to choose, start doing some research, look through books at your local library, go and listen to an orchestra play, attend a music or folk festival and be on the lookout for the right instrument for you.

Once you've decided, set yourself an intention to practice for half an hour every day and stick to it as best you can.

Find yourself a teacher if you'd like to learn from one. Discover and search out written material or music for your instrument.

If you already play an instrument choose to learn another one that has always been of interest to you.

Most of all have fun.

If you find that you're telling yourself "I'm not musical" turn that around into a positive statement, keep practising and before you know it the gift of playing music will be yours.

BUY A REBOUNDER

76

BUY A REBOUNDER

It's time to really energise your body.

Buy, hire or borrow a small circular trampoline commonly called a Rebounder or Lymphasizer. Do your best to find a good quality one and set it up in a pleasant surrounding.

By using one every day you will clear your lymphatic system and energise and oxygenate your whole body.

Begin by jumping up and down or running on the spot for 5 minutes and after a couple of days increase this to 10 minutes.

If it feels right, gradually increase this to 30 minutes for full aerobic effect.

You're jumping style can change every now and then to prevent boredom and it is important to breathe in time with your jumps.

Breathe in short sharp breaths one after the

other to the count of say 10 then breathe out the same way but breathe out a few more breaths than you breathed in. In this case you would do 12 or 13.

The use of weights to strengthen arm muscles can also be great once you're accustomed to the jumping.

Try taking a 20 or 30 minute walk following by 10 minutes lymphazing. You'll feel the difference in your body after a short time.

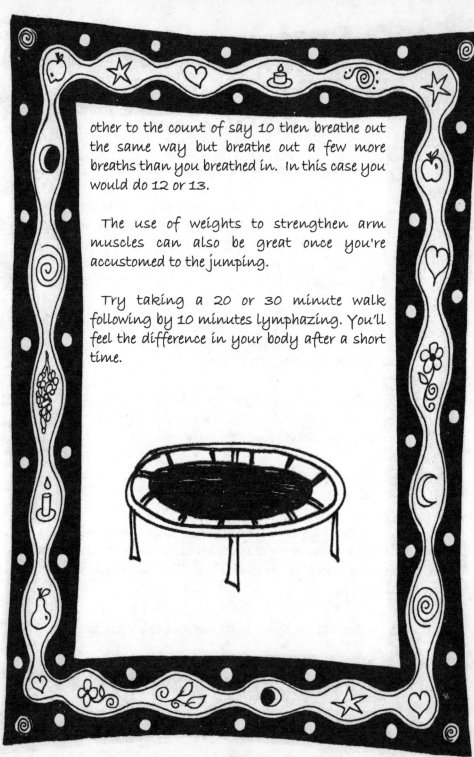

CREATE A SACRED GARDEN SCULPTURE

77

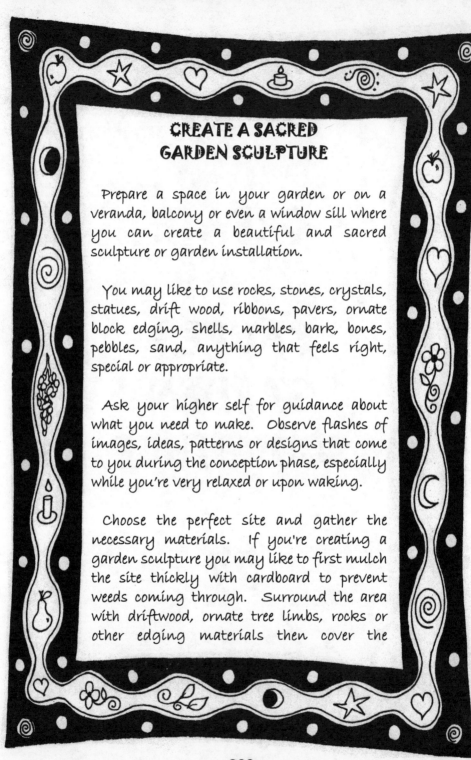

CREATE A SACRED GARDEN SCULPTURE

Prepare a space in your garden or on a veranda, balcony or even a window sill where you can create a beautiful and sacred sculpture or garden installation.

You may like to use rocks, stones, crystals, statues, drift wood, ribbons, pavers, ornate block edging, shells, marbles, bark, bones, pebbles, sand, anything that feels right, special or appropriate.

Ask your higher self for guidance about what you need to make. Observe flashes of images, ideas, patterns or designs that come to you during the conception phase, especially while you're very relaxed or upon waking.

Choose the perfect site and gather the necessary materials. If you're creating a garden sculpture you may like to first mulch the site thickly with cardboard to prevent weeds coming through. Surround the area with driftwood, ornate tree limbs, rocks or other edging materials then cover the cardboard with sand, barkchips, leaf mulch or similar base material.

Now place patterns of stones, crystals, shells etc on top of the base. Put a sculpture, ornament or piece of driftwood in the "right" place and enhance around it.

Create your own sacred sculpture in whatever way is perfect for you. Work with an intent if you feel to. Maybe you would like it to generate peace throughout your garden, home or the planet. Maybe it needs to help balance all the energies in its vicinity. It could be a symbol of abundance shared by all who live around it. The possibilities are endless. As you place each piece into the sculpture, know that you add energy to your intent with each placement.

Over time you will need to maintain your sculpture just as you do a garden bed. Take out any weeds that pop up and remove dead leaves and sticks if you feel the need to keep it clean and clear of clutter.

It is possible to create something similar yet

under cover if you don't have a garden or if you're renting and don't want to leave your beautiful creation behind.

You'll need some sort of flat bowl or container. The saucer from a large plant pot could be ideal or a big serving platter or bowl. Fill this with sand, pebbles or leaves and start from there.

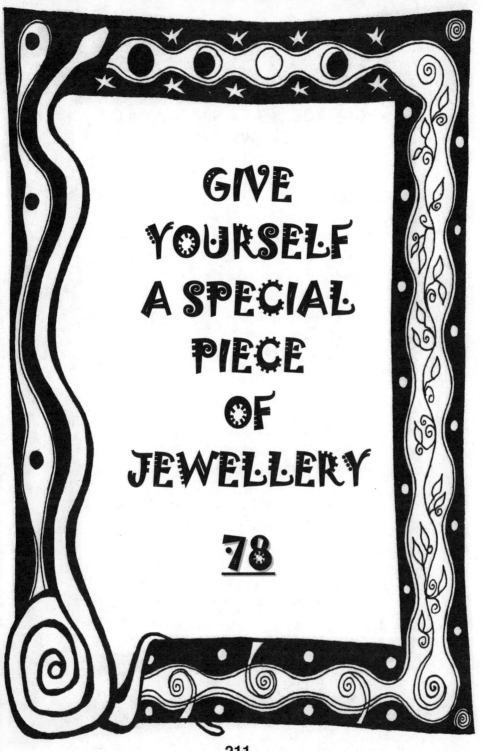

GIVE
YOURSELF
A SPECIAL
PIECE
OF
JEWELLERY

·78·

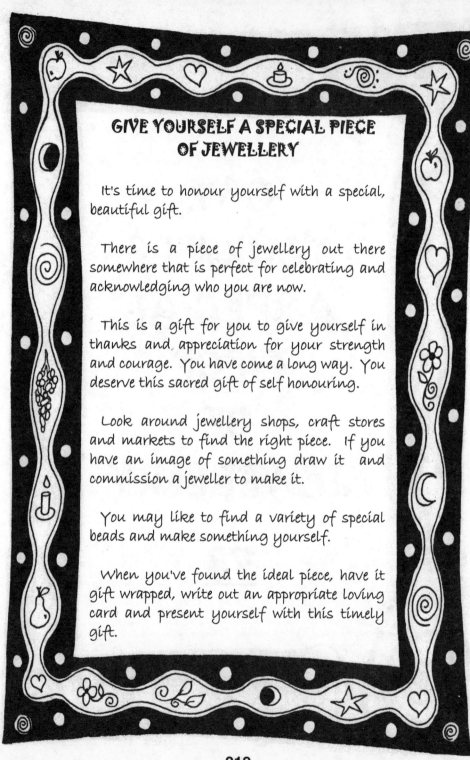

GIVE YOURSELF A SPECIAL PIECE OF JEWELLERY

It's time to honour yourself with a special, beautiful gift.

There is a piece of jewellery out there somewhere that is perfect for celebrating and acknowledging who you are now.

This is a gift for you to give yourself in thanks and appreciation for your strength and courage. You have come a long way. You deserve this sacred gift of self honouring.

Look around jewellery shops, craft stores and markets to find the right piece. If you have an image of something draw it and commission a jeweller to make it.

You may like to find a variety of special beads and make something yourself.

When you've found the ideal piece, have it gift wrapped, write out an appropriate loving card and present yourself with this timely gift.

YOUR VOICE IS A SWEET SWEET GIFT

·79·

YOUR VOICE IS A
SWEET SWEET GIFT

It's time to acknowledge that your voice is a gift that you can give to yourself as well as to others.

Maybe you were discouraged from singing as a child, or for some other reason feel you can't sing.

Everyone can sing and with a little help and encouragement you'll know you can too.

Choose songs that you enjoy singing, ones that are joyful, positive and that are within your voice range.

Treat yourself to a singing lesson. Learn harmonies or at the very least buy a music tape of healing chants and sing along as often as you can. Make up your own affirmations and sing them in a range that suits your voice.

Whenever you can and in whatever form is appropriate for you - sing, sing, sing.

PAINT YOUR YOUR INNER-SELF MANDALA

80

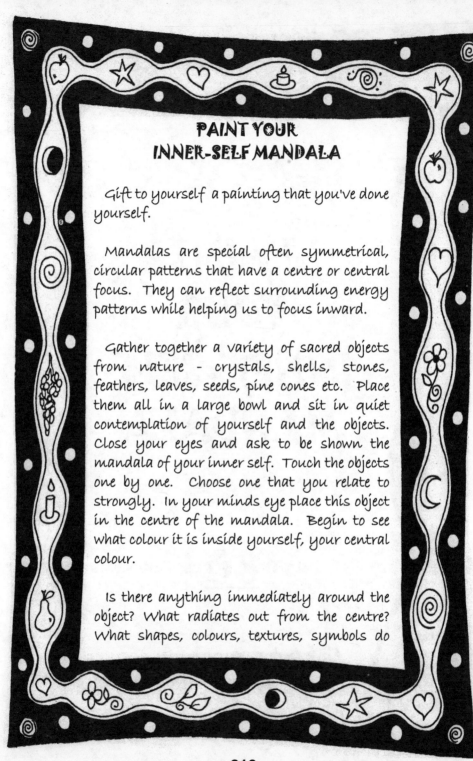

PAINT YOUR
INNER-SELF MANDALA

Gift to yourself a painting that you've done yourself.

Mandalas are special often symmetrical, circular patterns that have a centre or central focus. They can reflect surrounding energy patterns while helping us to focus inward.

Gather together a variety of sacred objects from nature - crystals, shells, stones, feathers, leaves, seeds, pine cones etc. Place them all in a large bowl and sit in quiet contemplation of yourself and the objects. Close your eyes and ask to be shown the mandala of your inner self. Touch the objects one by one. Choose one that you relate to strongly. In your minds eye place this object in the centre of the mandala. Begin to see what colour it is inside yourself, your central colour.

Is there anything immediately around the object? What radiates out from the centre? What shapes, colours, textures, symbols do you see? Is there a border or circle containing (or protecting) the whole picture?

Once you have the image strongly in your mind slowly open your eyes and make a pencil sketch of it, being sure to note the various colours.

Gather together or buy paints, brushes or crayons and either a canvas, special board or textured paper. (This process can also be done as a silk painting inside a hoop which can be decorated with feathers or tassels hanging down off the tensioning screw).

Mark it all out in pencil first. Take your time and begin creating your inner self mandala. Most of all enjoy the gift of your flowing creativity.

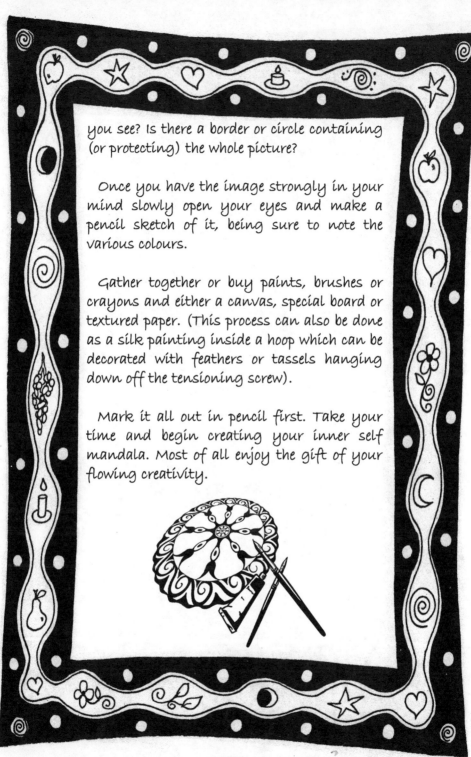

218

Thank You.

May LOVE, TRUTH and JOY

Be with you always.

MAY YOU MAKE THIS BOOK
A LIFESTYLE
AND GIVE YOURSELF LOVE,
PAMPERING,
AND MANY, MANY GIFTS
OFTEN.

CREDITS FOR ILLUSTRATIONS

JENNY KEMP - P's 74, 76, 79, 82, 89, 93, 95, 101, 103, 115, 175, 192, 195, 198, 217, 236

REBECCA HOPKINS - P's 31, 43, 47, 51, 99, 117, 138, 140, 143, 178, 186, 189, 200, 203, 205, 210, 221

ANDREW CLIFFORD (Reprinted from 'Manual For Teaching Permaculture Creatively' by Robin Clayfield and Skye) - P's 6, 33, 37, 39, 41, 59, 127

ANNETTE MULLER (Reprinted from 'You Can Have Your Permaculture And Eat It Too' by Robin Clayfield) - P's 87, 152

WILD, WONDERFUL WORDS and WISDOM.

(Book and resources that have inspired me and helped me grow.)

BOOKS

A Pattern Language. Christopher Alexander et al.
  (1977, Oxford University Press, U.S.A.)

At One With All Life. Judith L. Boice.
  (1989, Findhorn Press, Scotland)

Burnum Burnum's Aboriginal Australia. Burnum Burnum.
  (1988, Angus & Robertson, Australia)

Ceremonies for Change, Lynda S. Paladin.
  (1991, Stillpoint Publishing, U.S.A.)

Coming Back To Life. Joanna Macy.
  (1998, New Society publishers, Canada)

Conversations With God. Neale Donald Walsch.
  (1996, Hodder & Stoughton, Australia)

Creating Sacred Space With Feng Shui. Denise Linn.
  (1996, Piatkus, U.K.)

Creative Visualisation. Shakti Gawain.
  (1982, Bantam Books, U.K.)

Daughters of Copper Woman. Anne Cameron.
  (1984, The Women's Press Ltd, U.K.)

Despair and Personal Power in a Nuclear Age. Joanna Macy
  (1983, New Society Publishers, U.S.A.)

Earth Medicine. Jamie Sams.
  (1994, Harper Collins, U.S.A.)

Embracing The Beloved. Stephen and Ondrea Levine.
  (1996, Gateway Books, U.K.)

Endless Energy. Susannah and Leslie Kenton.
  (1993, Random House, U.K.)

Fit For Life. Harvey and Marilyn Diamond.
  (1985, Angus & Robertson, U.K.)

Flower Secrets Revealed. Carly Wall.
  (1993, A.R.E. Press. U.S.A.)

Forgiveness and Other Acts of Love. Stephanie Dowrick .
  (1997, Viking, Australia)

Good Grief Rituals. Elaine Childs-Gowell.
  (1992, Station Hill Press, U.S.A.)

Hands of Light. Barbara Ann Brennam.
  (1988, Bantam Books, U.S.A.)

Heal Your Body. Louise Hay.
  (1988, Specialist Publications, Australia)

Jaguar Woman. Lynne V. Andrews.
  (1985, Harper & Row, U.S.A.)

Laugh With Health. Manfred Urs Koch.
  (1981,Renaissance and New Age Creations, Australia.)

Living In the Light. Shakti Gawain.
  (1986, Pythagoren Press, Australia)

Maps To Ecstasy. Gabrielle Roth.
  (1989, New World Library, U.S.A.)

Medicine Woman. Lynne V. Andrews.
  (1981, Harper & Row, U.S.A.)

Passage To Power. Leslie Kenton.
  (1995, Edbury Press, U.K.)

Perelandra Garden Workbook. Machaelle Small Wright.
  (1987, Perelandra Ltd, U.S.A.)

Prospering Woman. Ruth Ross.
  (1995, New world Library, U.S.A.)

Serious Creativity. Edward de Bono.
  (1992, Mcquaig Group Inc, U.S.A.)

Song Of The Stone. Barry Brailsford.
  (1995, Stoneprint Press, N.Z.)

Star Woman. Lynne V. Andrews.
  (1986, Harper & Row, U.S.A.)

Succulent Wild Woman. Sark.
  (1997, Random House, U.S.A.)

The Artists Way. Julia Cameron.
  (1995, Pan Books, U.K.)

The Crone. Barbara G. Walker.
  (1985, Harper & Row, U.S.A.)

The Dance of Anger. Harriet Goldhor Lerner.
  (1985, Harper & Row, U.S.A.)

The Pathwork of Self-Transformation. Eve Pierrakos.
  (1990, Bantam Books, U.S.A.)

The Power Is Within You. Louise Hay.
  (1991, Specialist Publications, Australia)

The Seven Spiritual Laws of Success. Deepak Chopra.
  (1996, Bantam Press, U.K.)

The Spiral Dance. StarHawk.
  (1979, 1989. Harper SanFrancisco, U.S.A.)

Thinking Like A Mountain. John Seed, Joanna Macy, Pat Flemming,
Arne Naess.   (1988, New Society Publishers, U.S.A.)

Transforming Body Image. Marcia Germaine Hutchinson.
  (1985, The Crossing Press, U.S.A.)

Truth Or Dare. StarHawk.
  (1987, Harper SanFrancisco, U.S.A.)

You Can Have Your Permaculture and Eat It Too. Robin Clayfield.
  (1996, Earthcare Education, Australia)

Your Body's Energy. Emma Mitchell.
  (1998, Duncan Baird Publishers, U.K.)

When The Drummers Were Women. Layne Redmond.
  (1997, Random House, U.S.A.)

Wise women of the Dreamtime. K. Langloh Parker and Johanna Lambert.
  (1993, Inner Traditions International, U.S.A.)

Women Who Run With The Wolves. Clarissa Pinkola Estes.
  (1993, Random House, U.K.)

Women's Body, Women's Wisdom. Christiane Northrup M.D.
  (1998, Bantum Books, U.K.)

Working Out, Working Within. Jerry Lynch and Chungliang Al
Huang. (1998, Tarcher/Putnam, U.S.A.)

World as Lover, World as Self. Joanna Macy.
  (1991, Parallax Press, U.S.A.)

CARDS and PRINTED RESOURCES

(My favourites)

Creating Sacred Gardens-Knowledge Cards. Elizabeth Murray.
  (Pomegranate, U.S.A.)

Medicine Cards. Jamie Sams and David Carson.
  (1988, Bear & Co, U.S.A.)

Motherpeace (Cards and Book). Vicki Noble.
  (1983, Harper & Row, U.S.A.)

My Love Journal. Amber.
  (2001, Amber, 79 Crystal Waters, Maleny. 4552. Australia)

Oracle Of the Dreamtime (Cards and Book). Donni Hakanson.
  (2000, Connections Book Publishers, U.K.)

The Motherpeace Tarot Playbook. Vicki Noble and Jonathan Tenney.
  (1980, Wingbow Press, U.S.A.)

Wisdom Of The Four Winds (Cards and Book). Barry Brailsford.
  (1999, Stoneprint Press, N.Z.)

NETWORKING

(a small sample of events and products that I'd recommend)

WORKSHOPS, EVENTS, CONFERENCES

* Any of my workshops - I've included information fliers at the back.
* Heart Politics Conferences. Maleny Heart Politics, C\- Tracy Adams.
  P.O.Box 812, Maleny. Q'ld. 4552 or INTERHELP\Heart Politics,
  2 Terania St, The Channon. N.S.W. 2480
* Permaculture Courses. Directory advertised in 'The Planet' Journal. Russ
  Grayson (editor), P.O.Box 446, Kogarah. N.S.W. 2217 Ph.02 95886931
  <pacedge@magna.com.au>
* Deep Ecology. John Seed and Ruth Rosenheck, Rainforest Info. Centre,
  P.O.Box 368, Lismore. N.S.W. 2480 <johnseed1@ozemail.com.au>

* 'Stillness In Action' Retreats based around Meditation and action for world peace. P.O.Box 119, Bangalow. N.S.W. 2479. Ph. 02 6687 1789 <creative-edge@mail.com
* Aust. Institute of Body Electronics. Michelle Bell-Turner, P.O.Box 91, Yungaburra. Q'ld. 4872. Ph. 07 4095 2194 <michellebt@tpg.com.au>
* Breathconnection Rebirthing Intensives. 'Kaival Ya Meru', Kyogle Rd, Lillian Rock, N.S.W. 2480. Ph. 02 6689 7455.
* Wise Woman Healing Workshops + Camps, WorkShops and a Book for Teenagers. Amrita Hobbs, P.O.Box 337, Kyogle, N.S.W.2474 Ph. 0419336291.
* 'Urban Earth Motion' + other Dance and Movement Events and Rituals with Zjamal Xanitha. Ph. 07 5446 1448
* Vision Quests and Sweat Lodges with Peru. Lot 38, Crystal Waters, Maleny 4552. Ph. 07 5435 0203.
* Crystal Waters Permaculture Village (Visitors Camping Area, Village Tours etc). Barry O'Connell (Caretaker) Crystal Waters. Maleny. 4552 Ph. 07 5494 4726 or 07 5494 4620 (Co-op Office).
* Waterbreath Retreat (Watsu Therapy and Retreat Centre). 66 Crystal Waters, Maleny. 4552. Ph. 07 5494 4650
* Woodford Folk Festival. 27th Dec. to 1st Jan. each year. P.O.Box 1134, Woodford. 4514. Ph. 07 5496 1066
* The Kusun Study Tour for Percussion, Dance and Song with Nii Tettey Tetteh and Ray Pereira and local traditional musicians. 1 month long in Ghana, West Africa. C/- Jane Pentland, 17 McKillop St, Melbourne. 3000. Ph. 03 9670 5601 http:/rctvonline.net/percussion <janepentland@xcel.net.au>

GREAT PRODUCTS

* Chai Tea Mix. Annie Wall, 54 Crystal Waters, Maleny. 4552 Ph. 07 5494 4604
* Green Harvest (Organic Mail Order Supplies). 52 Crystal Waters, Maleny. 4552 Ph. 07 5494 4652
* Mukti Botanicals (Pure and Natural Eco-cosmetics). P.O.Box 747, Maleny. 4552 Ph. 07 5435 2111

Please send me your promotional material and I'll network it where I can. Use the following ads for my business as examples of what to send me.

EARTHCARE EDUCATION

Offering a diversity of Earth Healing, Teacher Training and Empowerment Courses, Workshops and Women's W'Ends as well as Publications, Resources and Tools for people wanting to learn and grow in a dynamic, creative, powerful and holistic way.

ROBIN CLAYFIELD

Robin has spent the past 23 years working, playing and interacting in groups in a variety of roles...
Facilitating and creating 1 and 2 week intensive residential courses, Training Teachers, Guiding Women's Weekends, Designing and Leading Empowerment and Visioning sessions for Community Groups, Businesses and Individuals, Lobbying Governments & Councils, Chairing Meetings, Presenting at Conferences, Living, Working and Sharing with others in Community... all in a spirit of empowerment, creativity and holistic growth and learning.

DYNAMIC GROUPS

AN ADVENTURE IN

CREATIVE FACILITATION

DESIGNED and CREATED FOR

Teachers and Facilitators
Activists and Earthworkers
Group and Workshop Leaders
Permaculture Teachers
Healers and Seminar Presenters

A one week intensive training to upskill people in the use and development of creative, interactive learning methods. Confidence, knowledge, creativity and tools are boosted in a dynamic, participatory and fun way.

HELD ONCE A YEAR AT CRYSTAL WATERS AND OCCASIONALLY AT OTHER VENUES AROUND THE WORLD. *I'M OPEN TO INVITATION.*

WILD WOMENS' WISDOM WEEKENDS

HEALING

CREATIVE PROCESSES

DANCE

FUN

GROWTH

SHARING

MUSIC

PASSION

FREEDOM

SUPPORT

RITUAL

HELD OVER A FULL WEEKEND
From Friday 5pm to Sunday 4pm.

With ROBIN CLAYFIELD & ZJAMAL XANITHA

HELD AT LEAST ONCE A YEAR ON THE SUNSHINE COAST (Q'ld, Aust.) IN A YUMMY PLACE OR AT A VENUE OF YOUR CHOICE IF YOU'D LIKE TO INVITE US.

AWAKEN YOUR DREAM

A 2 hour Visioning and Empowerment Process to support you to clear the way and step into what you really want to be doing in your life.   GO FOR IT - NOW !

CREATIVE FACILITATION CONSULTANT

and

KEYNOTE PRESENTER

for

Workshops, Seminars and Conference Sessions.

Designed to suit your Theme, Project or Audience.

RECHARGE

YOUR PROJECT
OR BUSINESS VENTURE

A ONE DAY WORKSHOP *USING CREATIVE, PRODUCTIVE AND INNOVATIVE PLANNING TOOLS.*

An 8 step process which helps you :

- *Turn problems into solutions*
- *Develop a positive vision*
- *See clearly your support networks*
- *Focus on your next step*
- *Develop tools for prosperity*
- *Give thanks, evaluate and celebrate where you are now.*

HELD WITHIN A 40 KM RADIUS OF MALENY OR AT YOUR INVITATION (ADD ON TRAVEL COSTS) IN OTHER LOCATIONS TO SUIT YOUR TIMING.

GIFTS FOR WILD WOMEN

A 3 HOUR PLAYSHOP AND EMPOWERMENT SESSION

GIVE YOURSELF THE MANY GIFTS THAT YOU DESERVE.

Feel Your Passion

Use Your Imagination and Spontaneity

Acknowledge and Connect with Spirit

Awaken Your Own Gifts

Honour your Connection to Earth and All Beings

Love Your Body, Mind and Spirit

Shed Your 'Stuff'

Eat Healthy Food

Think Loving Positive Thoughts

Hear Other Women's Stories

Manifest and Set Intentions

Express Thanks for Your Journey and the Gifts We Receive

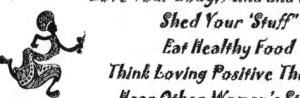

JOURNEY TO *Wholeness*

DUE FOR
RELEASE
LATE 2003

BY
ROBIN
CLAYFIELD

A *CD* of guided journeys set to music and sound

Relax With The Ocean

Trance Dance To Let It All Go

Breathe In The Universe

Living Earth Meditation

Step Into Your Dream

A Gift Just For You